Alfred's Christmas Sing-Along

60 of the World's Most Popular and Best Loved Traditional and Contemporary Christmas Songs

Selected and Arranged by Roger Edison

for Easy Piano and Voice with Optional Chord Symbols for Guitar

This comprehensive collection of Christmas music includes not only traditional favorite hymns and carols like *Silent Night, Adeste Fideles* and *Jingle Bells,* it also includes popular hits such as *The Christmas Song (Chestnuts Roasting on an Open Fire), I'll Be Home for Christmas, Jingle Bell Rock, Let It Snow! Let It Snow! Let It Snow!, Santa Claus Is Comin' to Town,* and *Winter Wonderland.*

Younger folks will enjoy *Rudolph, the Red-Nosed Reindeer, The Little Drummer Boy* and *Frosty the Snowman.* Christmas songs that bring a smile include *All I Want for Christmas Is My Two Front Teeth,* and the hilarious country hit *Grandma Got Run Over by a Reindeer.*

Classical music is represented by excerpts from *The Nutcracker, Gesú Bambino* and *The Ukrainian Bell Carol.* And crowning the Christmas season are two selections for the New Year. Here are 60 of the very best songs written about the holiday season, for easy piano and voice, with optional chord symbols for guitar. We know this will soon become your favorite Christmas book of all!

Alfred Music
P.O. Box 10003
Van Nuys, CA 91410-0003
alfred.com

D1465962

ISBN-10: 0-7390-4273-4
ISBN-13: 978-0-7390-4273-1

Contents

If you were to compile a list of the best-loved Christmas songs written in the last 50 years or so, this one would be on most everyone's list. Written by crooner Mel Tormé (The Velvet Fog) and his friend Robert Wells, the song evokes heartwarming images of the things we associate with the holiday season. Nat Cole's creamy-smooth rendition, recorded in 1946, has established the song as a Christmas perennial.

Words only, p. 128

The Christmas Song
(Chestnuts Roasting on an Open Fire)

Lyric and Music by
Mel Tormé and Robert Wells

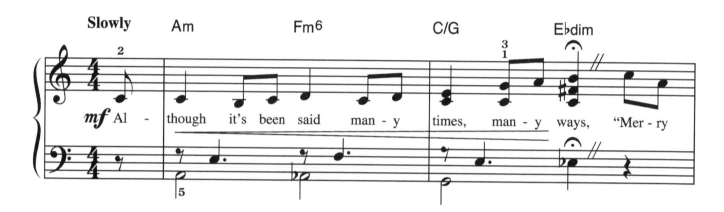

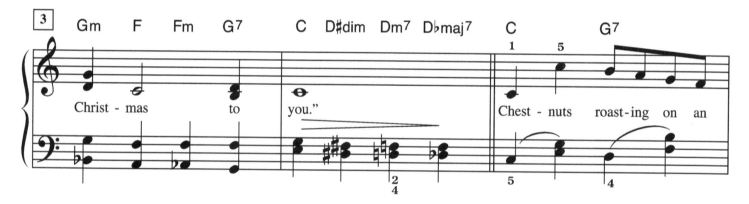

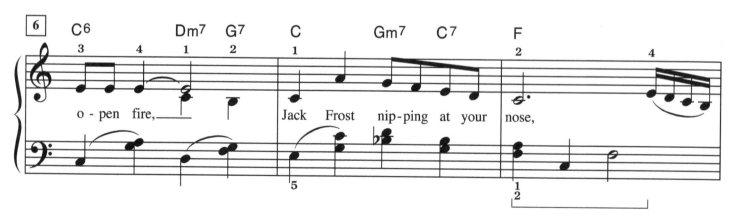

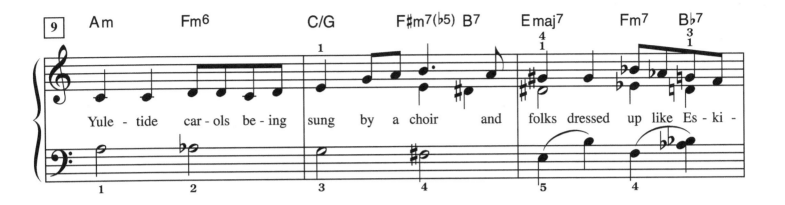

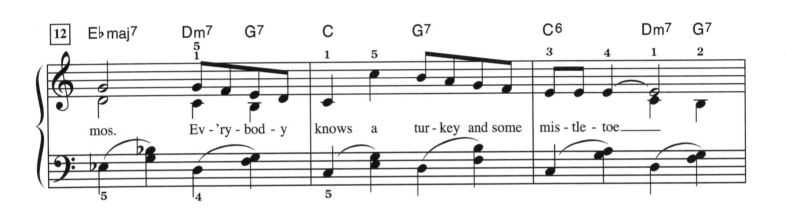

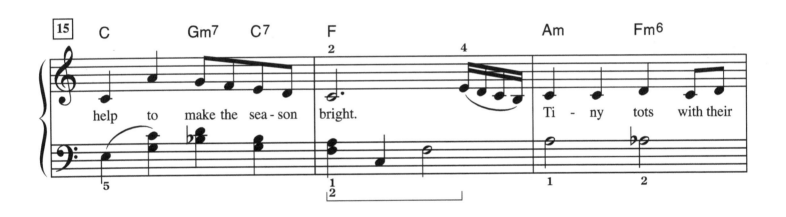

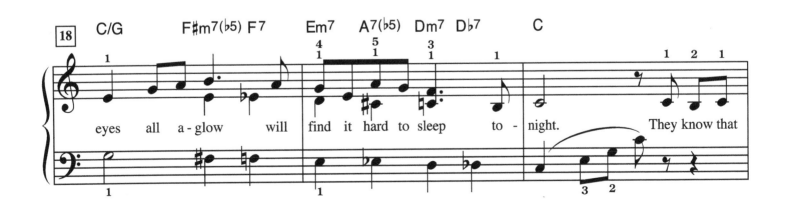

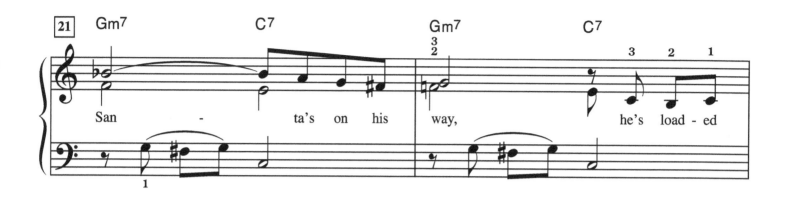

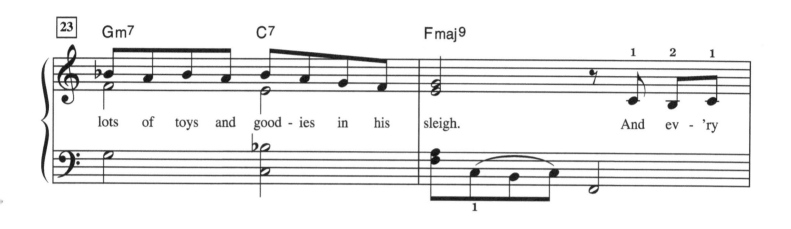

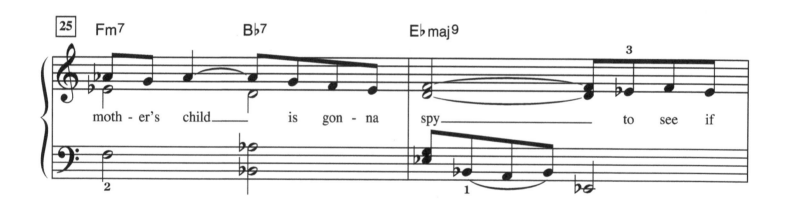

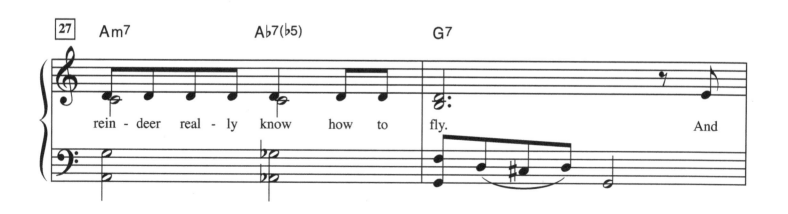

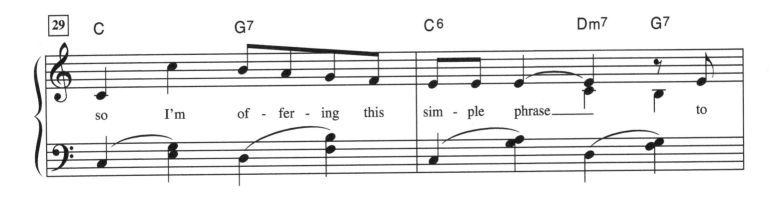

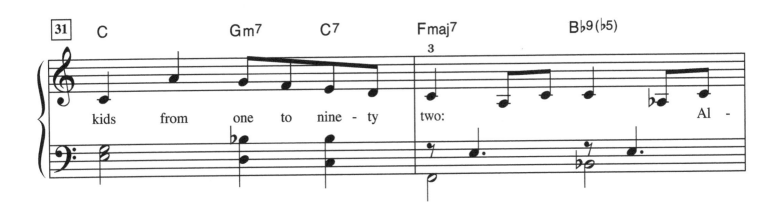

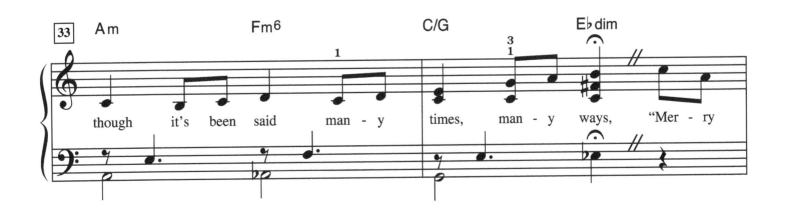

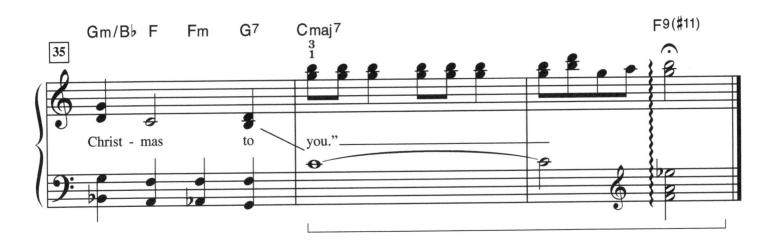

Similar to the old tearjerker, "M-O-T-H-E-R," this song also uses each letter of its spelled-out title as inspiration for the lyrics that follow. This song has a simple melody with heartfelt lyrics, and recordings of the piece became hits for country music stars Eddy Arnold and Jim Reeves.

Words only, p. 128

C-H-R-I-S-T-M-A-S

Words and Music by
Eddy Arnold and Jenny Lou Carson

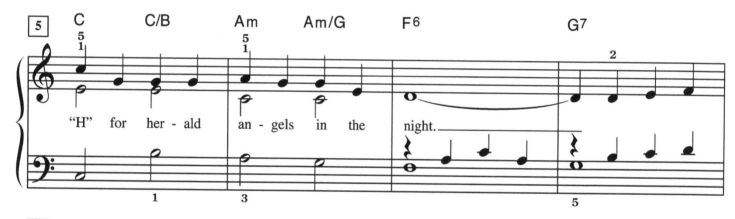

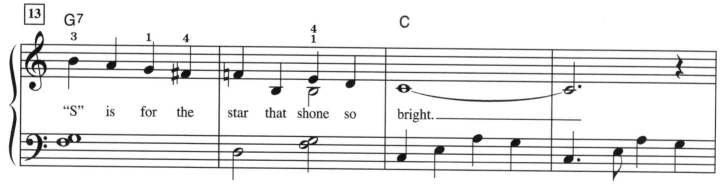

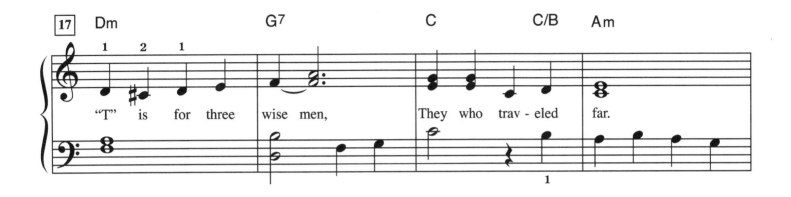

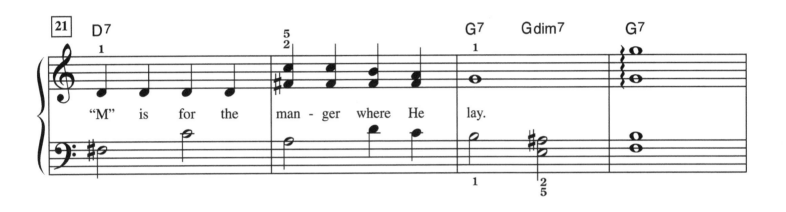

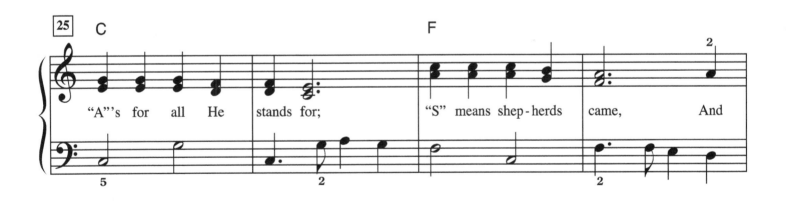

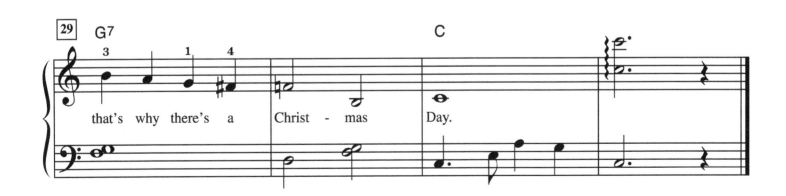

Who doesn't love snowmen and sleigh bells? Nobody, that's who! Written by music business pros Felix Bernard and Dick Smith, *Winter Wonderland* dates from 1934, but it took hit recordings by Perry Como and The Andrews Sisters in 1946 to establish the song as a Christmas standard.

Words only, p. 128

Winter Wonderland

Words by Dick Smith

Music by Felix Bernard

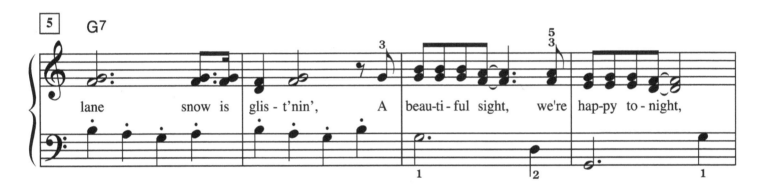

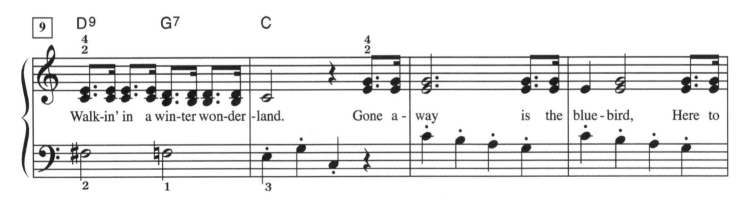

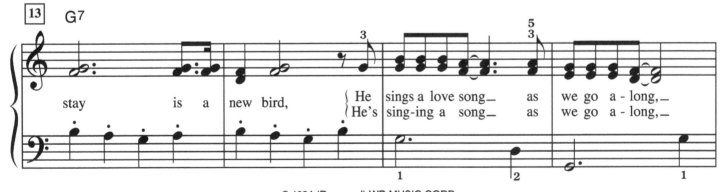

In 1932, songwriters Haven Gillespie and J. Fred Coots came up with the idea of a song that told about a Santa Claus who rewarded good children but passed the naughty ones by. Not a single publisher was interested, but the writers finally persuaded Eddie Cantor to perform the song on his radio show. It became an instant hit and was later recorded by virtually every famous singer of the time.

Words only, p. 128

Santa Claus Is Comin' to Town

Words by Haven Gillespie

Music by J. Fred Coots

The 1944 Hollywood movie *Meet Me in St. Louis* tells the story of an average American family that goes to the 1904 World's Fair. The score is full of great songs, including "The Trolley Song," "The Boy Next Door," and this one, "Have Yourself a Merry Little Christmas," all sung by the immortal Judy Garland.

Words only, p. 129

Have Yourself a Merry Little Christmas

Words and Music by
Hugh Martin and Ralph Blane

The famous songwriting team of Sammy Cahn and Jule Styne had one of their biggest hits with this Christmas song from 1945. When someone told Cahn that they thought "let it snow" was a common English expression and therefore couldn't be copyrighted, he replied, "Maybe once, maybe twice, but say it three times—and it's mine!"

Words only, p. 129

Let It Snow! Let It Snow! Let It Snow!

Words by Sammy Cahn

Music by Jule Styne

It seems that songs that become popular during the stress of wartime come to have a more profound meaning. Such is the case with this lovely ballad, made popular by Bing Crosby's heartfelt rendition, recorded during World War II. The last two lines of the song had special meaning to many American GIs.

Words only, p. 129

 # I'll Be Home for Christmas

Lyrics by Kim Gannon

Music by Walter Kent

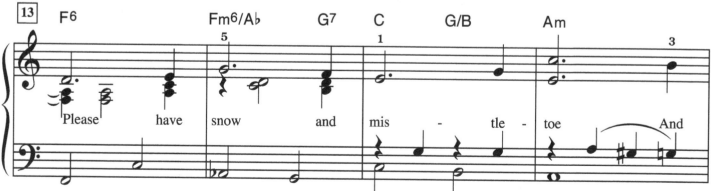

In this charming fable, a poor little drummer boy gives the Baby Jesus the only gift he can afford: a song on his drum. His gift is as appreciated as the rich gifts the Wise Men bring (not a bad lesson to remember in this day of seasonal overspending). Harry Simeone, one of the writers, made the song a hit in 1958 with his choral group.

Words only, p. 129

The Little Drummer Boy

Words and Music by
Katherine Davis, Henry Onorati
and Harry Simeone

After the phenomenal success of "Rudolph the Red-Nosed Reindeer" in 1949, songwriter Johnny Marks started his own publishing company, named it "St. Nicholas Music," and started turning out more Christmas songs. This song dates from 1964 and was sung by Burl Ives on a television Christmas special.

Words only, p. 130

A Holly Jolly Christmas

**Words and Music by
Johnny Marks**

Have a hol - ly jol - ly Christ-mas, it's the best time of the year.

I don't know if there'll be snow, but have a cup of cheer. Have a

hol - ly jol - ly Christ-mas, and when you walk down the street

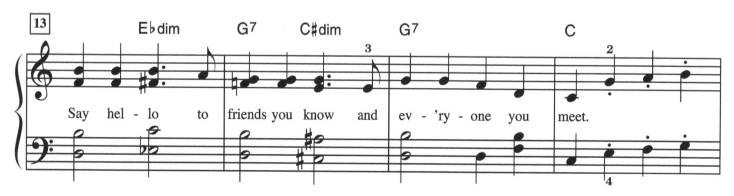

Say hel - lo to friends you know and ev - 'ry - one you meet.

The polka is based on a peasant dance that originated in Bohemia (now the Czech Republic) in the 1830s. The name comes from the Czech word *pulka* (half), which refers to the characteristic short steps of the dance. The polka's popularity spread all over the world, especially to parts of the U.S. that house people of Central European origin. The Andrews Sisters' 1939 smash hit recording of "Beer Barrel Polka" (based on a Czech polka) ensured its continuing popularity in America. Burke and Webster wrote this Christmas polka in 1949.

Words only, p. 130

The Merry Christmas Polka

Words and Music by
Sonny Burke and Paul Webster

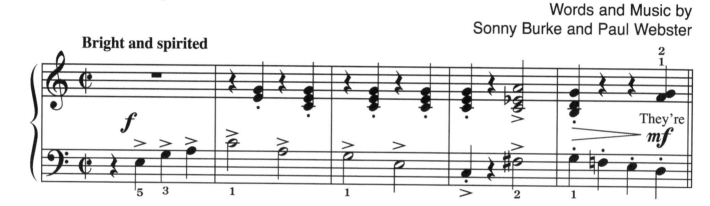

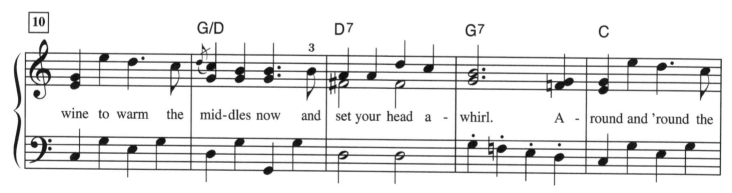

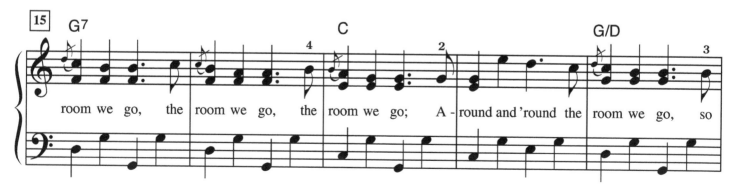

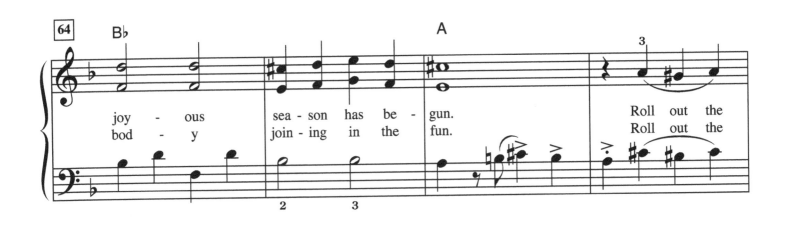

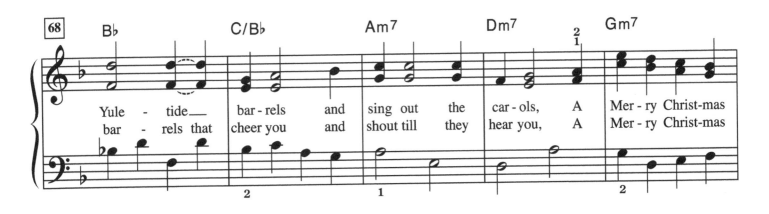

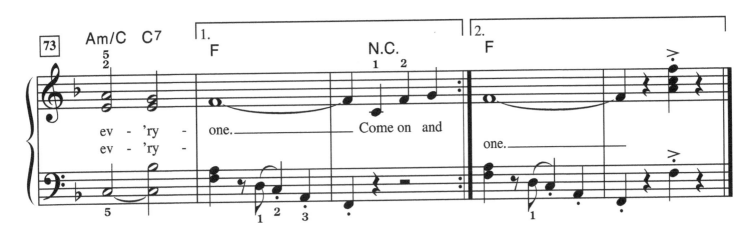

This piece is a product of songwriting team Mickey J. Addy (a composer of many Christmas favorites) and lyricist Carl Sigman, who is also responsible for dozens of hits including "What Now My Love," "It's All in the Game," "The Twelfth of Never," "Ebb Tide," "Pennsylvania 6-5000," and "Where Do I Begin (Love Story)."

Words only, p. 130

There Is No Christmas Like a Home Christmas

Words by Carl Sigman

Music by Mickey J. Addy

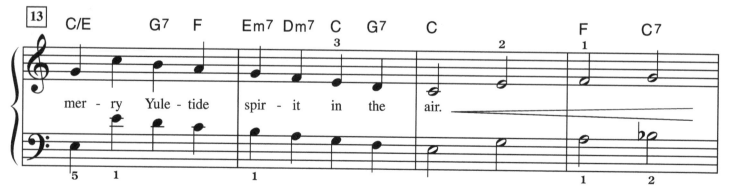

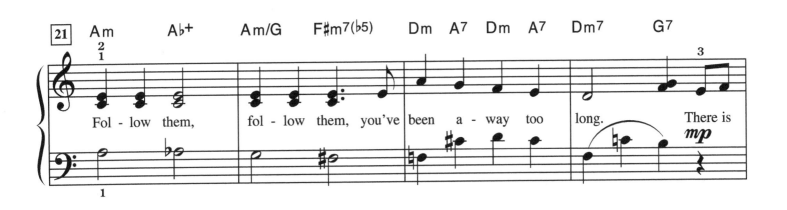

Bing Crosby had the hit on this Christmas confection back in 1949. The song was written by business pro's Carl Sigman (words) and Peter De Rose (music).

Words only, p. 130

A Marshmallow World

Words by Carl Sigman

Music by Peter De Rose

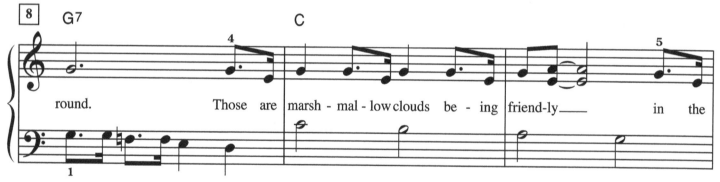

The songwriting team of Sammy Kahn and Jule Styne was responsible for innumerable hit songs. Among these hits are "Three Coins in the Fountain," "I'll Walk Alone," jazz standard "Time After Time," and "Let It Snow! Let It Snow! Let It Snow!" (also in this collection). This piece dates from 1954 and was written at the request of Frank Sinatra.

Words only, p. 131

 # The Christmas Waltz

Words by Sammy Cahn

Music by Jule Styne

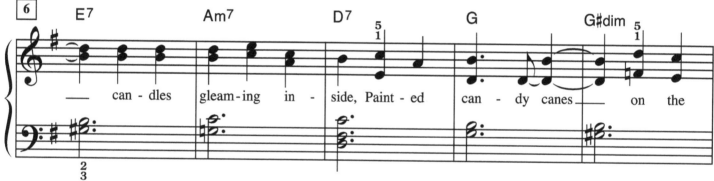

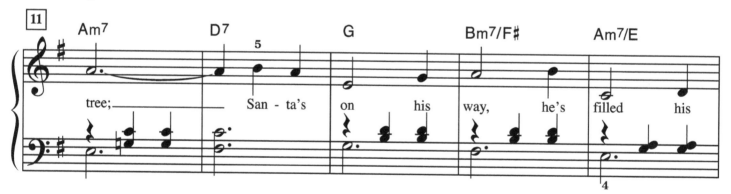

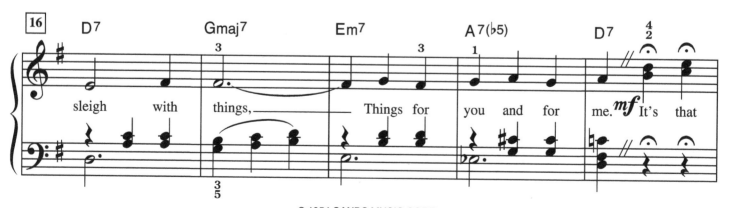

The idea of setting a Christmas song to the rhythm of an Irish jig occurred to three Irish songwriters back in the 1950s. They came up with this spirited song, which became a big hit for Irish tenor Dennis Day in 1951. Killarney is a lovely town in the southwest part of Ireland.

Words only, p. 131

Christmas in Killarney

Words and Music by
John Redmond, James Cavanaugh
and Frank Weldon

neigh-bors pay a call. And Fa - ther John be-fore he's gone will bless the house and all. How

grand it feels to click your heels and join in the fun of the jigs and reels; I'm

hand - ing you no blar - ney, the likes you've nev - er known is

Christ-mas in Kil-lar-ney with all of the folks at home. The all of the folks at home.

Who can argue with the sentiments expressed in this happy Christmas waltz? Kids and jingle bells, friends coming to call, parties and caroling... even the scary ghost stories (no doubt a reference to Charles Dickens' *A Christmas Carol*) leave everyone happy. Songwriters Eddie Pola and George Wylie penned this upbeat tune in 1963.

Words only, p. 131

It's the Most Wonderful Time of the Year

Words and Music by
Eddie Pola and George Wylie

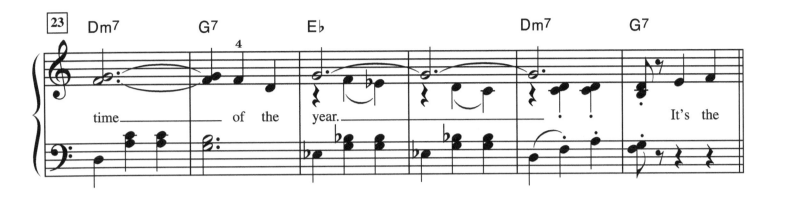

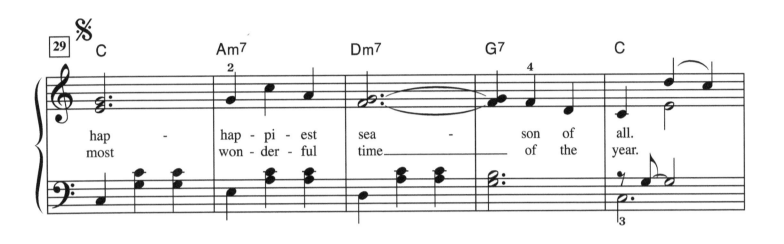

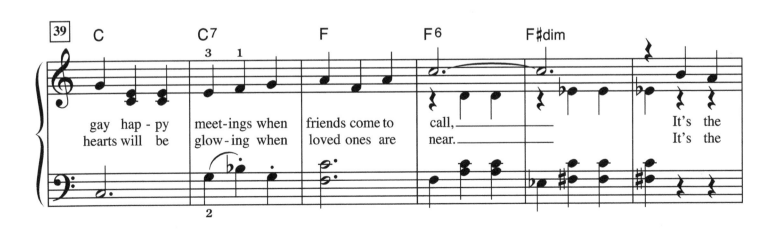

Just before Christmas in 1818, an Austrian village priest named Father Joseph Mohr noticed that the church organ had been damaged by mice and was unplayable. Needing something to sing on Christmas Eve, he dashed off some words and gave them to his organist, Franz Gruber, asking him to compose a melody that could be accompanied by a few simple guitar chords. From its first performance on that Christmas Eve till today, the quiet beauty of *Silent Night* has brought joy to millions of people.

Words only, p. 132

Silent Night

Words by Joseph Mohr

Music by Franz Gruber

Original German words:
Stille nacht, heilige nacht!
Alles schlaft, einsam wacht
Nur das traute, hochheilige Paar,

Holder Knabe im lockigen Haar,
Schlaf in himmlischer Ruh'
Schlaf in himmlischer Ruh'.

Although he came from a famous, wealthy family, James Pierpont was something of a rebel. Much to the horror of his abolitionist father, he espoused the Confederate cause before the Civil War, and even moved to the South. Pierpont wrote many songs, but is remembered only for this one. The song was actually written for Thanksgiving under the title "The One-Horse Open Sleigh," but the Christmas-like jingle bell rhythm of the chorus proved irresistible, and the song went on to become the best-known Christmas song in the world.

Words only, p. 132

Jingle Bells

Words and Music by
James Pierpont

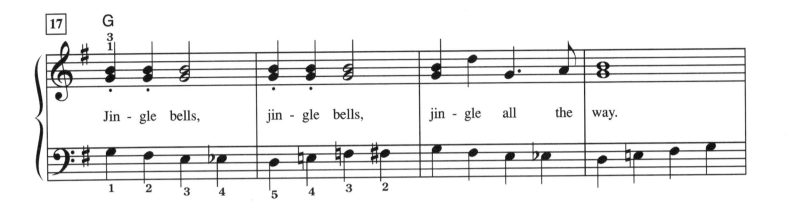

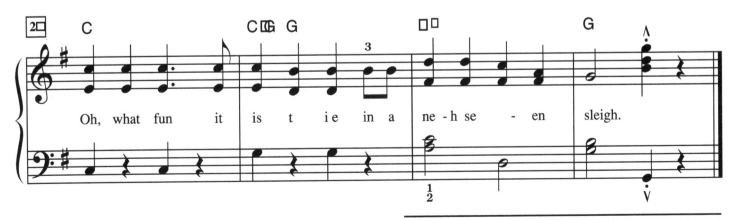

One of the most popular carols of all time, this one comes from several sources. The melody of the first part is derived from an 18th-century popular song. The words are a translation of a French Carol, *Les anges dans nos campagnes (Angels in Our Countryside)*. The famous refrain, "Gloria in excelsis Deo" is thought to date from the Middle Ages. The carol was first published in its present form in 1855.

Words only, p. 132

Angels We Have Heard on High

Traditional

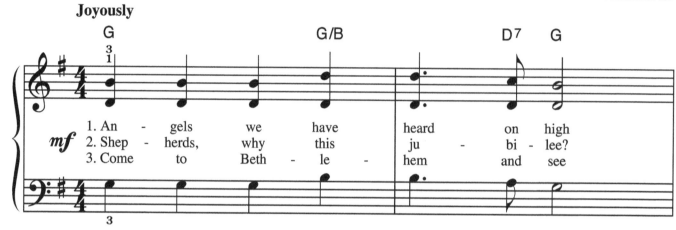

1. An - gels we have heard on high
2. Shep - herds, why have this ju - bi - lee?
3. Come to Beth - le - hem and see

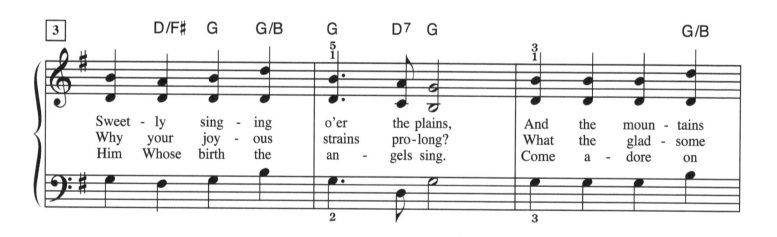

Sweet - ly sing - ing o'er the plains, And the moun - tains
Why your joy - ous strains pro - long? What the glad - some
Him Whose birth the an - gels sing. Come a - dore on

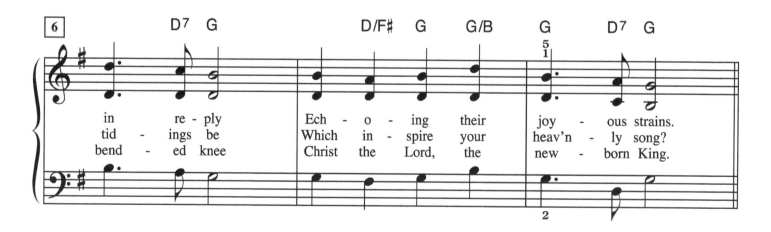

in re - ply Ech - o - ing their joy - ous strains.
tid - ings be Which in - spire your heav'n - ly song?
bend - ed knee Christ the Lord, the new - born King.

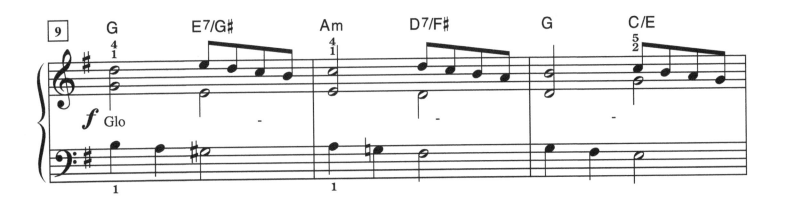

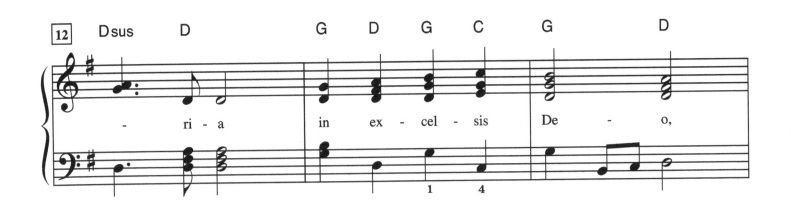

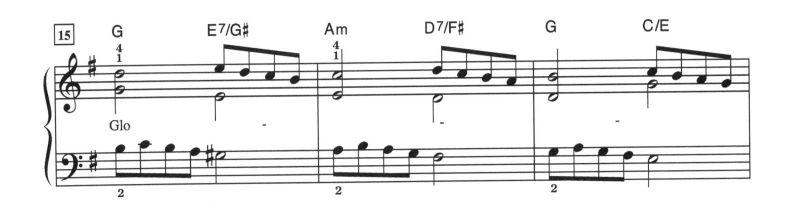

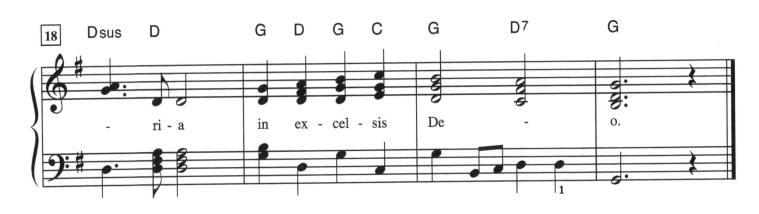

Before Christianity reached Britain, pagan tribes had long been decorating their dwellings with holly boughs as a protection against evil spirits. With the arrival of Christianity the tradition continued, with the holly symbolizing Christ's death and resurrection. Even today the holly's red berries and green leaves are the traditional colors of the holiday. The original Welsh words were about New Year's night; the familiar American words printed here date from the 1880s.

Deck the Hall

Words only, p. 132

Traditional Welsh Carol

Brightly, with spirit

1. Deck the hall with boughs of hol - ly, Fa la la la la la la la la.
2. See the blaz - ing Yule be - fore us, Fa la la la la la la la la.
3. Fast a - way the old year pass - es, Fa la la la la la la la la.

'Tis the sea - son to be jol - ly, Fa la la la la la la la la.
Strike the harp and join the cho - rus, Fa la la la la la la la la.
Hail the new, ye lads and lass - es, Fa la la la la la la la la.

Don we now our gay ap - par - el, Fa— la, fa— la, la la la.
Fol - low me in mer - ry meas - ure, Fa— la, fa— la, la la la.
Sing we joy - ous all to - geth - er, Fa— la, fa— la, la la la.

Troll the an - cient Yule - tide car - ol, Fa la la la la la la la la.
While I tell of Yule - tide treas - ure, Fa la la la la la la la la.
Heed - less of the wind and weath - er, Fa la la la la la la la la.

Until the Civil War, white America had pretty much ignored African-American music. However, during the war, several white officers of black regiments wrote down the melodies they heard the soldiers singing. The first collection of these songs was published in 1867. Shortly after that, an African-American choral group called the Fisk University Jubilee Singers made many of these melodies, now known as spirituals, widely known.

Words only, p. 132

Go, Tell It on the Mountain

African-American Spiritual

Noël is the French word for Christmas. On *la nuit avant Noël* (the night before Christmas) French children wait for *Bonhomme Noël* (Old Man Christmas) who leaves toys and sweets on the hearth for children who have been good. For the naughty ones, bogeyman *Père Fouettard* leaves a bundle of switches for punishment. The first complete version of this carol in English dates from 1833.

Words only, p. 133

The First Noel

Traditional

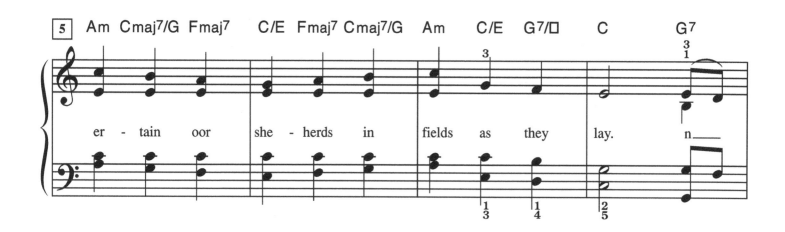

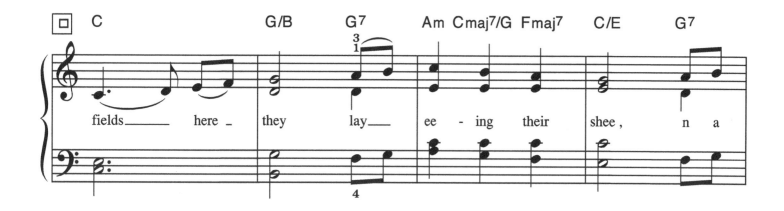

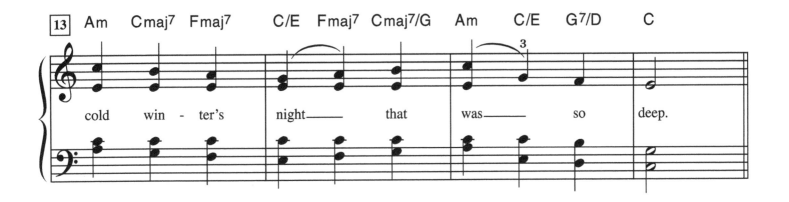

cold win - ter's night_____ that was_____ so deep.

Chorus:

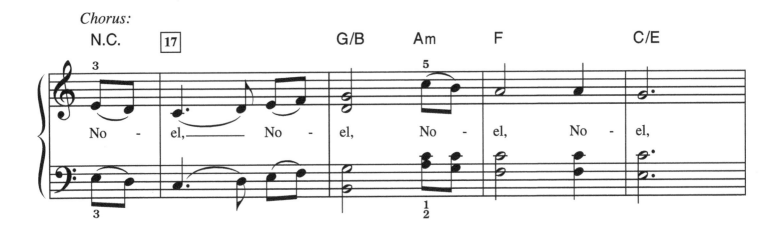

No - el,_____ No - el, No - el, No - el,

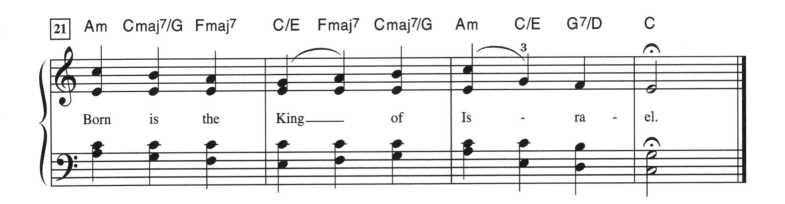

Born is the King_____ of Is - ra - el.

2. They looked up and saw a star,
   Shining in the East beyond them far;
   And to the earth it gave great light,
   And so it continued day and night.
   (Chorus)

3. This star drew nigh to the northwest;
   O'er Bethlehem it took its rest,
   And there it did both stop and stay,
   Right o'er the place where Jesus lay.
   (Chorus)

4. Then entered in those Wise Men three,
   Full rev'rently upon their knee,
   And offered there in His presence
   Their gold and myrrh and frankincense.
   (Chorus)

This is a very old carol. The word "ye" is an archaic form of the plural of "you." The word "rest" means "keep." Therefore, the title means "May God Keep You Merry, Gentlemen." The music is written in the medieval Aeolian mode in D (D E F G A B♭ C D). The song was first published in 1827 and was well known to Charles Dickens, who mentions it in his famous book, *A Christmas Carol*.

Words only, p. 133

God Rest Ye Merry, Gentlemen

Traditional

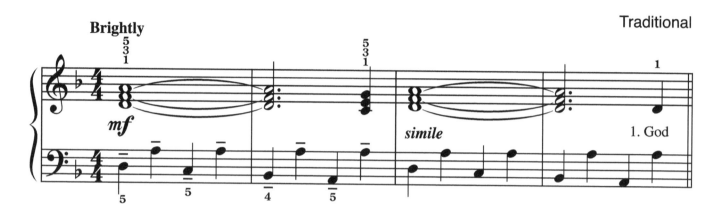

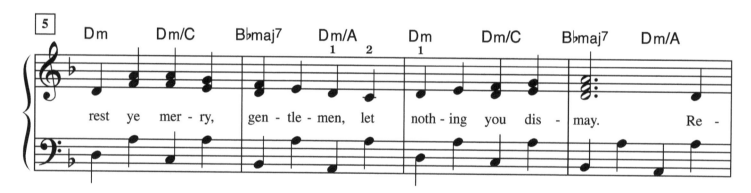

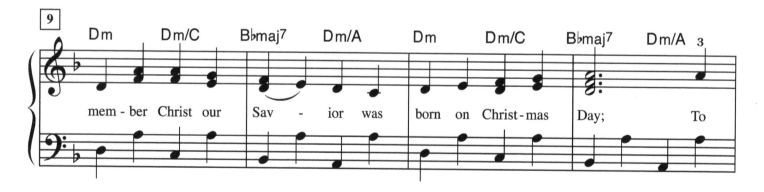

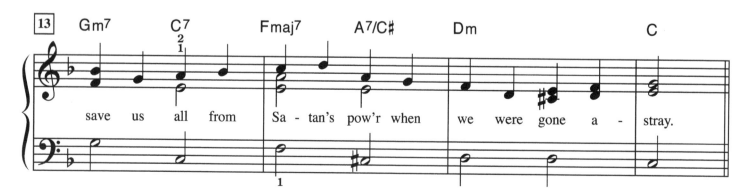

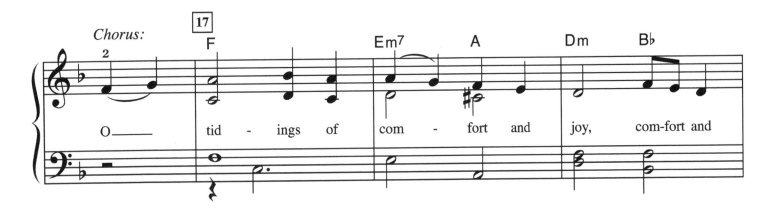

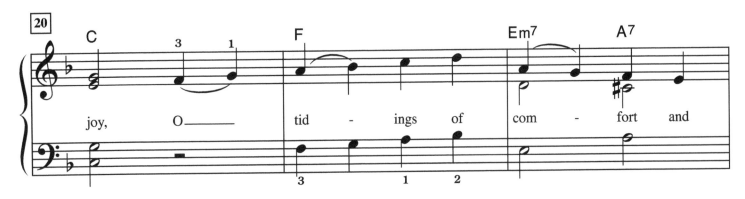

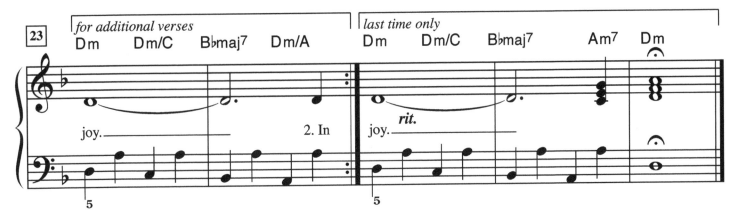

2. In Bethlehem in Jewry this blesséd Babe was born,
   And laid within a manger upon this blesséd morn;
   To which His mother Mary did nothing take in scorn.
   (Chorus)

3. From God our heavenly Father a blesséd angel came,
   And unto certain shepherds brought tidings of the same,
   How that in Bethlehem was born the Son of God by name.
   (Chorus)

4. "Fear not," then said the angel, "Let nothing you affright;
   This day was born a Savior of a pure Virgin bright
   To free all those who trust in Him from Satan's power
   and might."
   (Chorus)

5. The shepherds at those tidings rejoicéd much in mind
   And left their flocks a-feeding in tempest, storm and wind,
   And went to Bethlehem straightaway this blesséd Babe to find.
   (Chorus)

6. But when to Bethlehem they came where at this Infant lay,
   They found Him in a manger where oxen feed on hay;
   His Mother Mary kneeling unto the Lord did pray.
   (Chorus)

7. Now to the Lord sing praises, all you within this place,
   And with true love and brotherhood each other now embrace;
   This holy tide of Christmas all others doth deface.
   (Chorus)

Wenceslas was a real king who lived in Bohemia (now part of the Czech Republic) about 1,000 years ago. He earned a reputation for kindness and generosity, but was murdered by a jealous younger brother. In 1853 an American priest, John Mason Neale, was given a collection of church and school songs, which included a 13th-century Latin song called *Tempus adest floridum (Spring Has Unfolded Her Flowers)*. He wrote new words and published the result—the carol we know as "Good King Wenceslas."

Words only, p. 134

 # Good King Wenceslas

Traditional

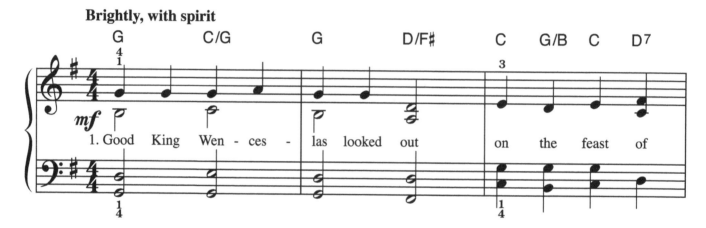

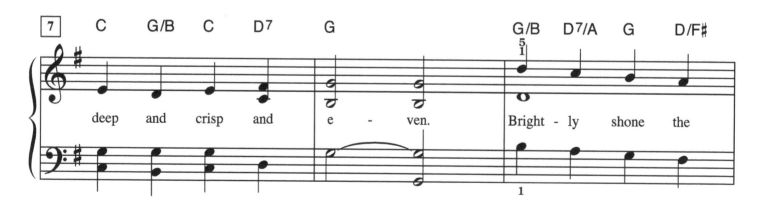

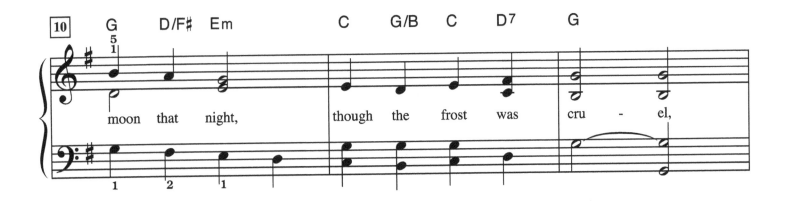

moon that night, though the frost was cru - el,

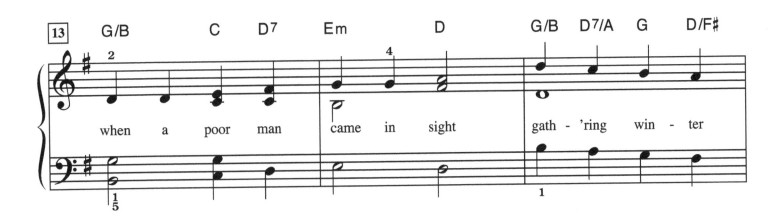

when a poor man came in sight gath - 'ring win - ter

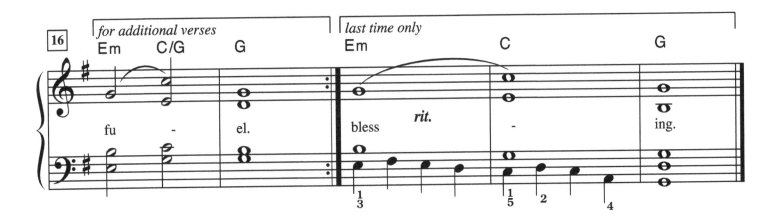

for additional verses

fu - el.

last time only

bless *rit.* - ing.

2. "Hither, page, and stand by me,
   If thou know'st it, telling,
   Yonder peasant, who is he?
   Where and what his dwelling?"
   "Sire, he lives a good league hence
   Underneath the mountain,
   Right against the forest fence,
   By Saint Agnes' fountain."

3. "Bring me flesh and bring me wine,
   Bring me pine logs hither:
   Thou and I will see him dine
   When we bear them thither."
   Page and monarch, forth they went,
   Forth they went together
   Through the rude wind's wild lament
   And the bitter weather.

4. "Sire, the night is darker now
   And the wind blows stronger;
   Fails my heart, I know not how
   I can go no longer."
   "Mark my footsteps, good my page,
   Tread thou in them boldly;
   Thou shalt find the winter's rage
   Freeze thy blood less coldly."

5. In his master's steps he trod
   Where the snow lay dinted;
   Heat was in the very sod
   Which the Saint had printed.
   Therefore, Christian men be sure
   Wealth or rank possessing,
   Ye who now will bless the poor
   Shall yourselves find blessing.

Felix Mendelssohn was only 17 when his delightful overture to Shakespeare's *A Midsummer Night's Dream* established him as a genius in the European musical world. In his short life of only 38 years, Mendelssohn went on to write a huge amount of music of every type, including an 1840 choral work that celebrated the invention of printing. Some of this music was later adapted to words by Charles Wesley, brother of the man who founded Methodism. The hymn has become a favorite in Great Britain and the United States, even though Mendelssohn himself thought it unsuitable for a sacred text.

Words only, p. 134

 # Hark! The Herald Angels Sing

Words by Charles Wesley

Music by Felix Mendelssohn

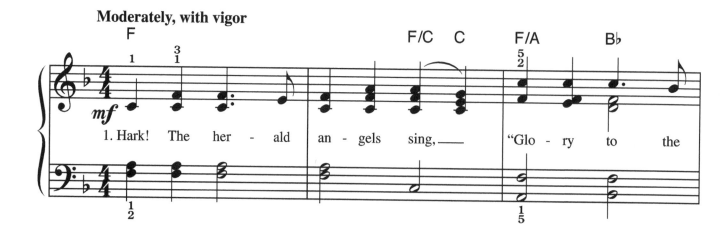

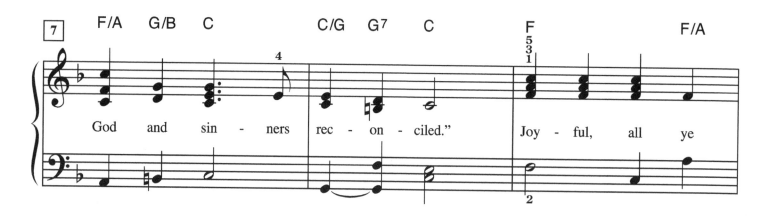

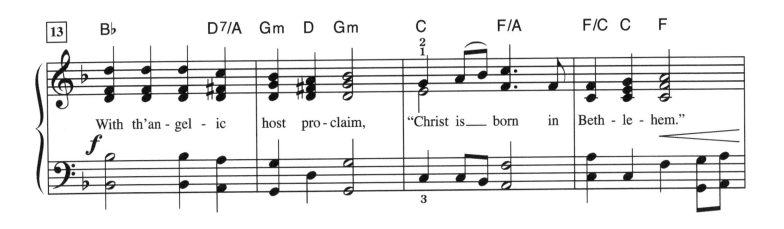

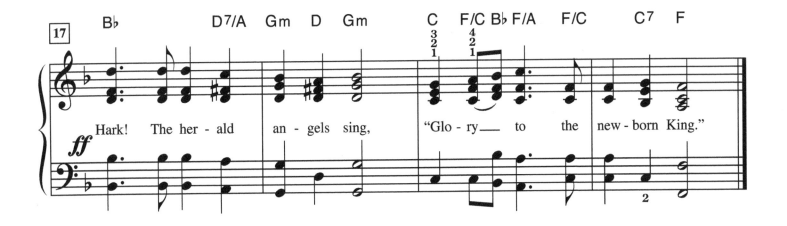

2. Christ, by highest heav'n adored,
   Christ the everlasting Lord,
   Late in time behold Him come,
   Offspring of the Virgin's womb!
   Veiled in flesh the Godhead see;
   Hail th'incarnate Deity!
   Pleased as Man with men to dwell,
   Jesus, our Immanuel,
   Hark! The herald angels sing,
   "Glory to the newborn King."

3. Hail the heav'n-born Prince of Peace!
   Hail the Sun of Righteousness!
   Light and life to all He brings,
   Ris'n with healing in His wings.
   Mild He lays His glory by,
   Born that man no more may die,
   Born to raise the sons of earth,
   Born to give them second birth.
   Hark! The herald angels sing,
   "Glory to the newborn King."

Many years ago in England, bands of roving musicians called *waits* roved the streets during the holiday season, singing and playing in the hopes of earning a pudding, a drink, or a few pennies. This song, also called "The Wassail Song," was a popular waits carol of the time. "Wassail" was a drink made with ale or wine spiced with roasted apples and sugar. The word comes from an old Anglo-Saxon toast, "waes hael," which means "be healthy."

Words only, p. 134

Here We Come A-Caroling
(The Wassail Song)

Traditional

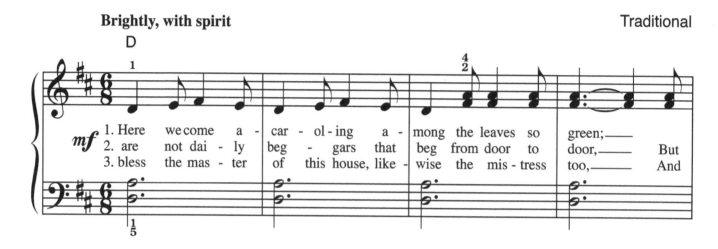

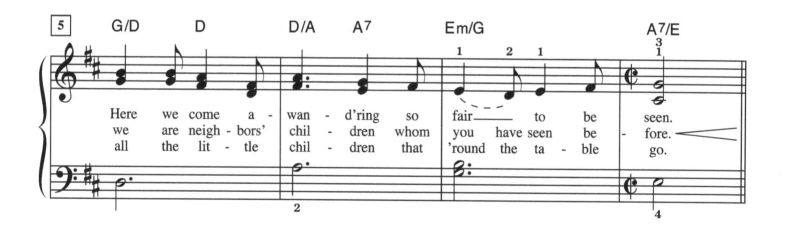

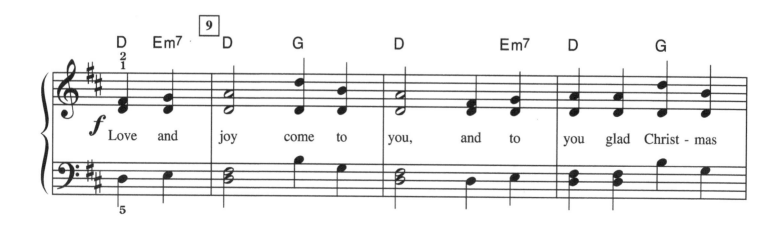

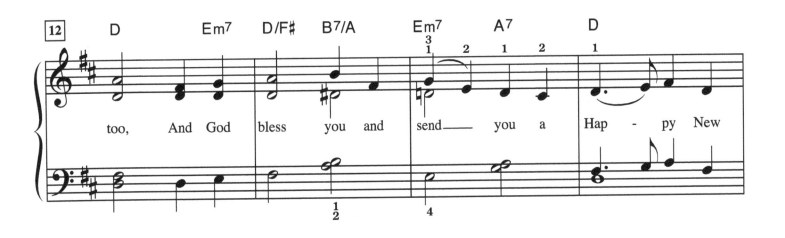

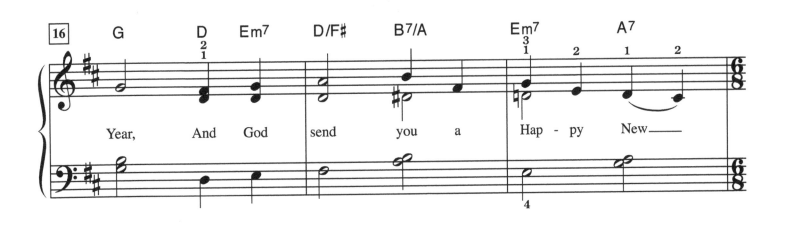

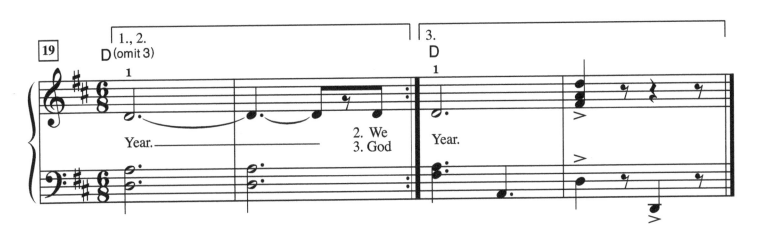

The Bible makes no mention of either the Virgin Mary or the Baby Jesus ever having set foot on a ship. And, of course, Bethlehem is nowhere near the sea. Nevertheless, this carol depicting Mary and Jesus on a ship has been sung for over 300 years, and is as popular as ever.

Words only, p. 135

I Saw Three Ships

Traditional

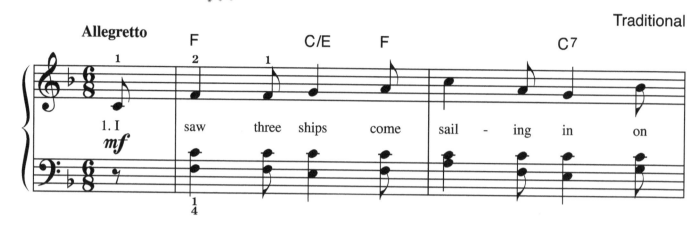

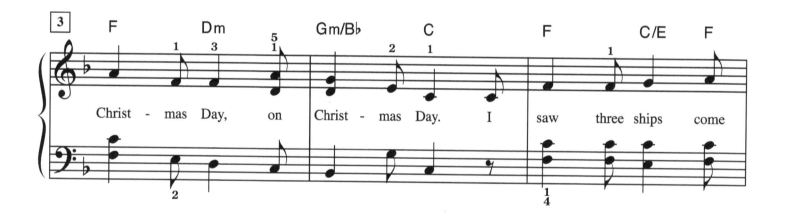

2. And what was in those ships all three,
   On Christmas Day, on Christmas Day?
   And what was in those ships all three,
   On Christmas Day in the morning?

3. Our Savior Christ and His Lady…
   (continue similarly)

4. Pray, whither sailed those ships all three?…

5. O, they sailed into Bethlehem…

6. And all the bells on earth shall ring…

7. And all the angels in Heav'n shall sing…

8. And all the souls on earth shall sing…

9. Then let us all rejoice amain…

The original St. Nicholas was a 4th-century bishop in Asia Minor (present-day Turkey), who was credited with having miraculous powers. During a famine, he promised sailors that if they gave their ships' cargo of grain to feed the townspeople, they would find their ships miraculously refilled. Sure enough, the miracle was fulfilled and the sailors became his first converts. Nicholas eventually became the patron saint of many countries, including the Netherlands. The Dutch brought traditions associated with St. Nicholas to the New World, especially to New York City, which was a Dutch colony until 1664. It was here in the New World that St. Nicholas became known as Santa Claus.

Words only, p. 135

Jolly Old St. Nicholas

Traditional

Unitarian minister Edmund Hamilton Sears wrote the deeply felt words of this hymn in 1849. Sears had a vision of an era of world peace that could only be attained through the coming of Christ. This hymn is often sung to a tune by Arthur Sullivan (of Gilbert and Sullivan fame), but the melody more familiar to Americans is this one, penned by Boston-born composer Richard S. Willis (1819–1900).

Words only, p. 135

It Came Upon the Midnight Clear

Words by Edmund Hamilton Sears

Music by Richard S. Willis

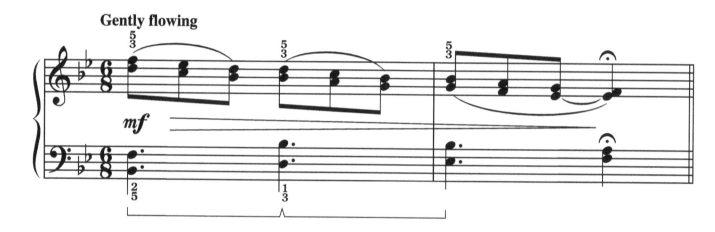

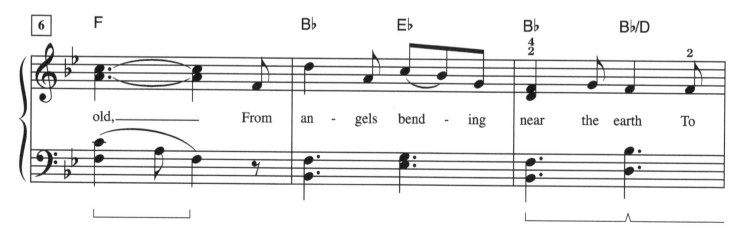

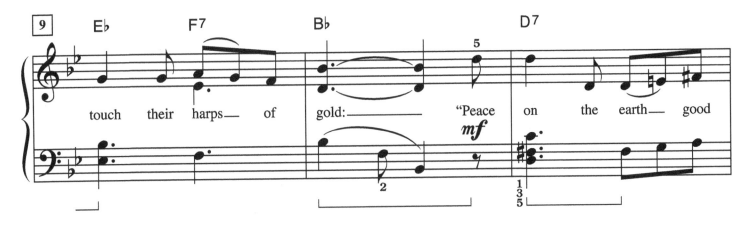

touch their harps— of gold:———————— "Peace on the earth— good

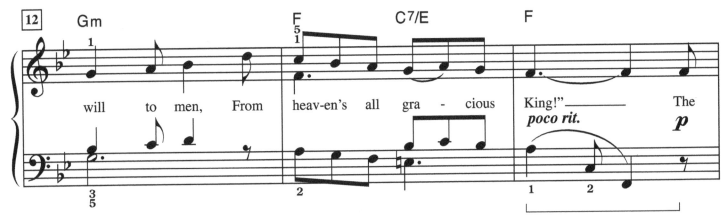

will to men, From heav-en's all gra - cious King!"——————— The

world in sol - emn still - ness lay To hear the an - gels sing.———

2. Still through the cloven skies they come with peaceful wings unfurled,
   And still their heavenly music floats o'er all the weary world:
   Above its sad and lowly plains they bend on hovering wing,
   And ever o'er its Babel sounds the blessed angels sing.

3. Yet with the woes of sin and strife the world has suffered long;
   Beneath the heavenly strain have rolled two thousand years of wrong;
   And man, at war with man, hears not the tidings which they bring;
   O hush the noise, ye men of strife and hear the angels sing.

4. O ye, beneath life's crushing load, whose forms are bending low
   Who toil along the climbing way with painful steps and slow.
   Look now! for glad and golden hours come swiftly on the wing;
   O rest beside the weary road and hear the angels sing!

5. For lo! the days are hastening on, by prophet bards foretold,
   When with the ever-circling years comes round the age of gold;
   When peace shall over all the earth its ancient splendors fling,
   And the whole world send back the song which now the angels sing.

When young Isaac Watts complained to his minister father that the hymns they sang in church were of inferior quality, his father challenged him to write better ones. By the following Sunday, Isaac had turned out the first of hundreds of beautiful lyrics that he would write during his lifetime. *Joy to the World* comes from his 1719 collection *The Psalms of David, Imitated.* Fully 120 years later, American music teacher Lowell Mason set the words to music. Because he used themes from *Messiah,* Mason modestly gave credit to his idol, composer George Frideric Handel.

Words only, p. 136

Joy to the World

Words by Isaac Watts

Music by Lowell Mason
(after George Frideric Handel)

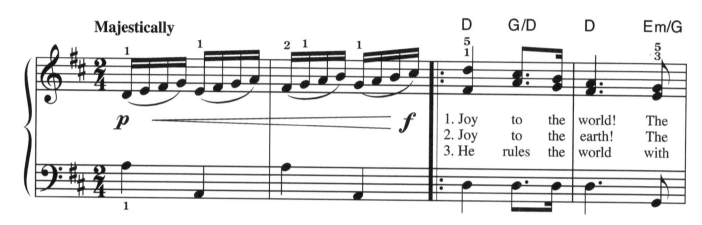

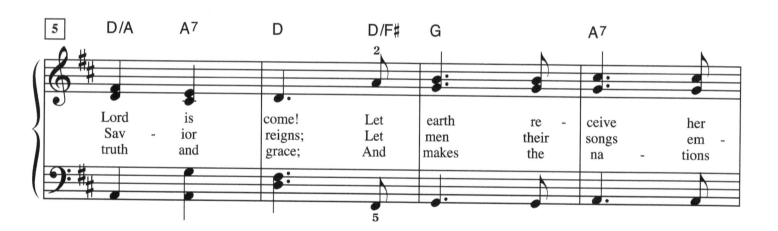

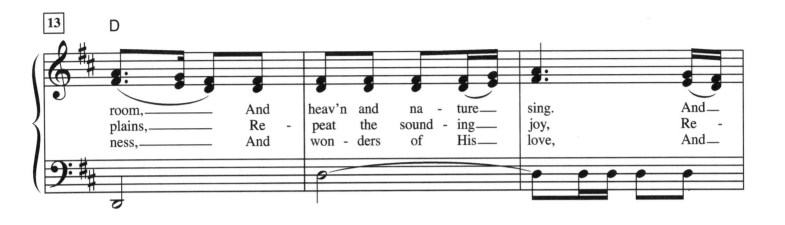

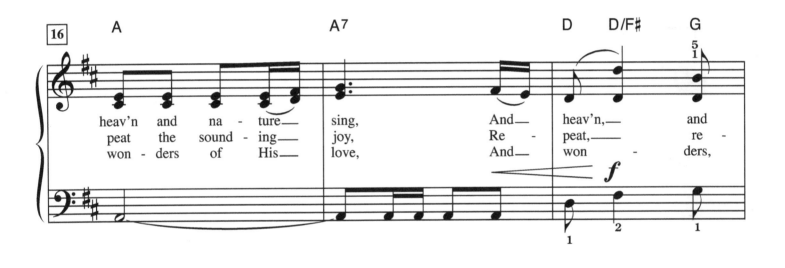

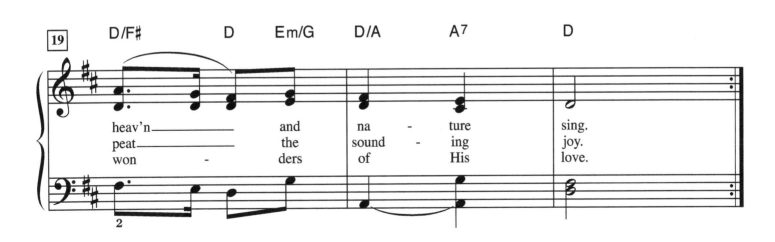

Hundreds of years before the birth of Jesus, the rose was associated with Aphrodite, the Greek goddess of love. According to legend, a bee stung Aphrodite's son Cupid when he stopped to smell a rose. Enraged, he shot an arrow into the bush, which is how the rose acquired its thorns. During the Middle Ages, many Christian cults that worshipped the Virgin Mary sprang up. Some cults assigned her the attributes of the rose, symbolic of perfect love. In this serene German carol from 1599, Mary is the rose and Jesus is her blossom.

Words only, p. 136

 # Lo, How a Rose E'er Blooming

Words: 15th-century German Carol

Music by Michael Praetorius

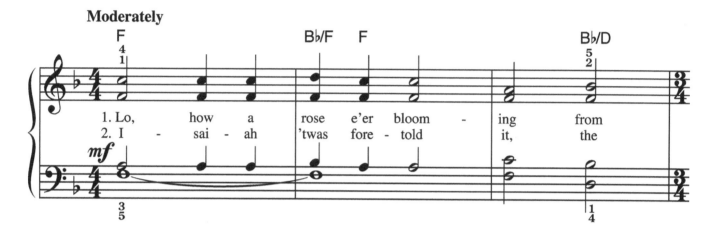

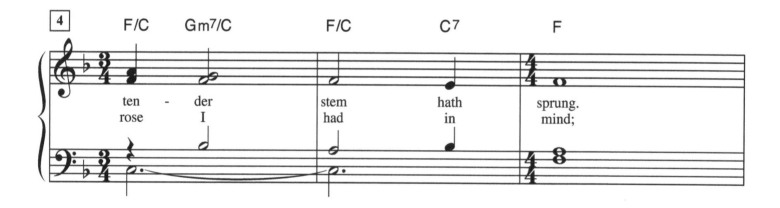

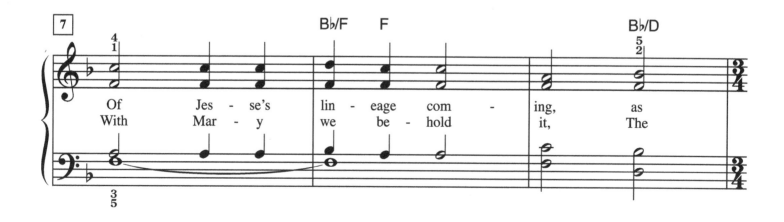

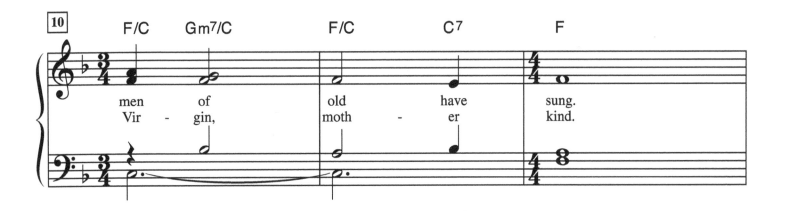

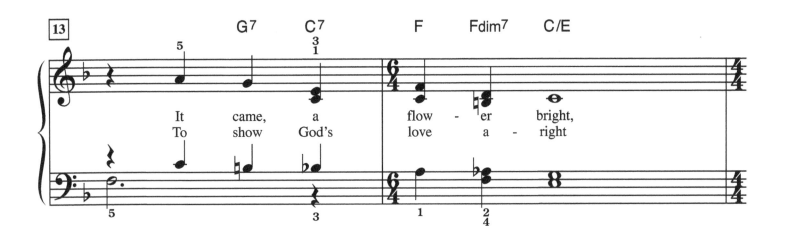

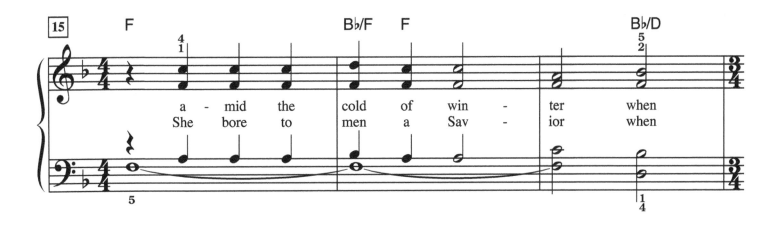

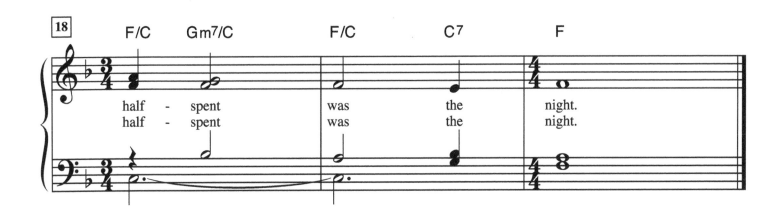

Decorating a Christmas tree at holiday time was originally a German practice, but in the last 200 or so years, the custom has spread all over the world. The melody of *O Christmas Tree* is an old German folk song, first published in 1799. Subsequently, many sets of words have been written for this tune, including the college song "Lauriger Horatius" and the great rallying song of the Confederacy "Maryland, My Maryland."

Words only, p. 136

O Christmas Tree

(O Tannenbaum)

Traditional German Carol

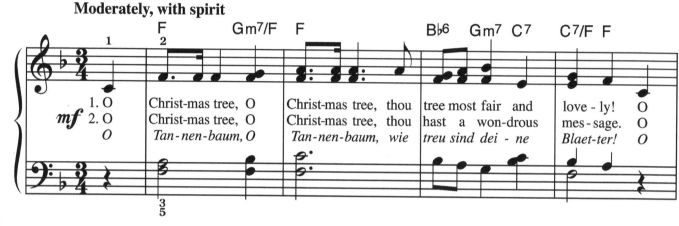

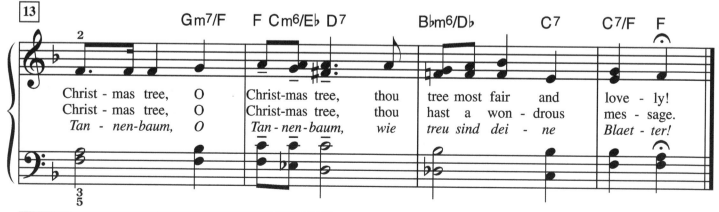

One of the reasons we picture Santa Claus as we do is because of C. C. Moore's famous 1822 poem, "A Visit from Saint Nicholas," also known as "The Night Before Christmas." In the poem are the eight tiny reindeer, the jolly old Santa Claus, and his rooftop method of delivering Christmas presents. *Up on the Housetop* was written a few years after Moore's poem became popular.

Words only, p. 136

Up on the Housetop

Words and Music by
Benjamin Hanby

John Francis Wade was an Englishman who lived in France in the 18th century. He is credited as the author of both the Latin words and the melody of this beloved hymn; however, some authorities believe the melody predates Wade. Frederick Oakeley, a Catholic priest who eventually became Canon of Westminster, translated the words into English in 1852.

Words only, p. 136

O Come, All Ye Faithful
(Adeste Fideles)

Latin words by John Francis Wade
English translation by Frederick Oakeley

Music by John Francis Wade

Brightly

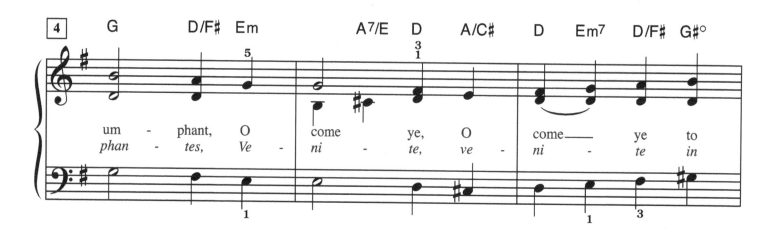

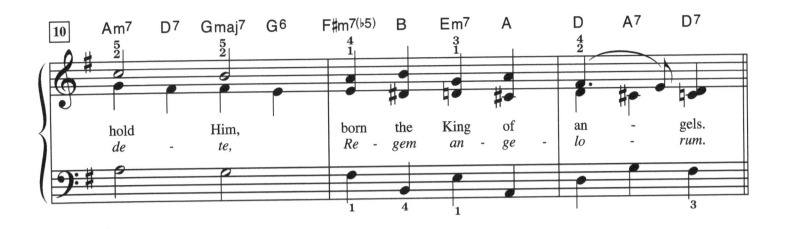

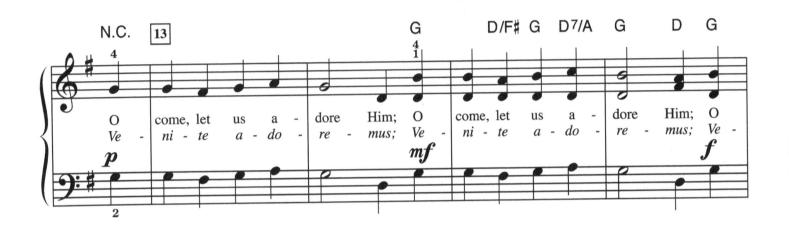

2. Sing, choirs of angels,
   Sing in exultation;
   Sing all ye citizens of heav'n above.
   Glory to God, all glory in the highest.
   O come, let us adore Him;
   O come, let us adore Him;
   O come, let us adore Him, Christ, the Lord.

3. Yea, Lord, we greet Thee,
   Born this happy morning;
   Jesus, to Thee be all glory giv'n;
   Word of the Father, now in flesh appearing.
   O come, let us adore Him;
   O come, let us adore Him;
   O come, let us adore Him, Christ, the Lord.

Millions of people revere the serenely beautiful melodies originally called Latin plainsong. These chants date back to a time before music had accompanying chords, a steady beat, or any kind of definite notation. Plainsong was already ancient when Pope (later Saint) Gregory had hundreds of them written down about 1,500 years ago. In his honor we call them Gregorian chants. The music of this carol is plainsong, but over the years, writers and arrangers have added modern chords, measured notation and a lovely set of English words. Emmanuel, a poetic name for Jesus, comes from the Hebrew "God is with us."

Words only, p. 137

 # O Come, O Come, Emmanuel

English lyrics by John M. Neale

13th-century Plainsong

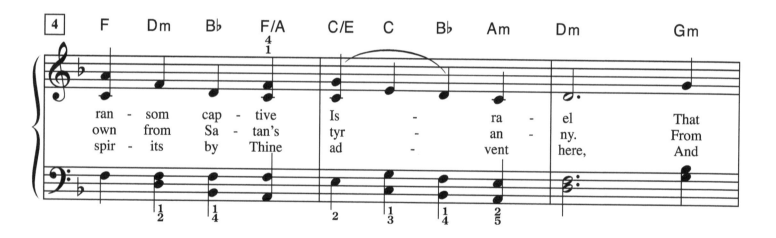

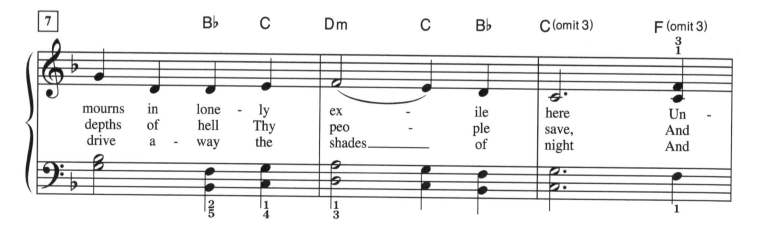

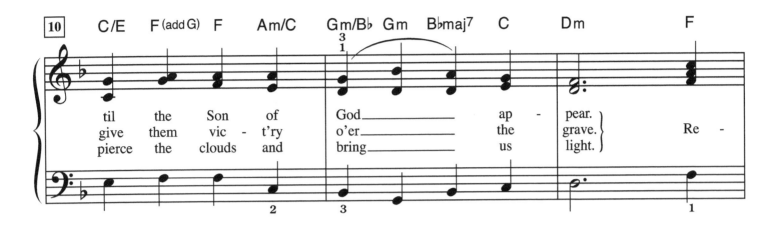

til the Son of God appear.
give them vic - t'ry o'er the grave.
pierce the clouds and bring us light.

Re -

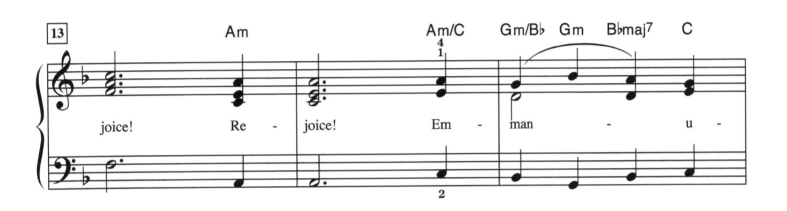

joice! Re - joice! Em - man - u -

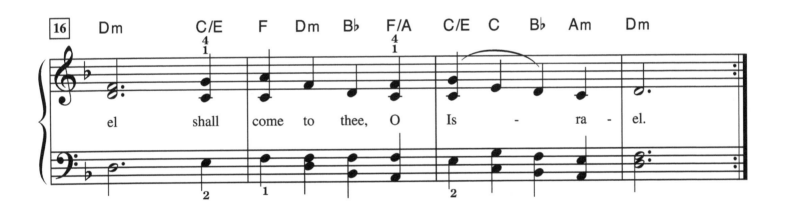

el shall come to thee, O Is - ra - el.

Slowly and deliberately

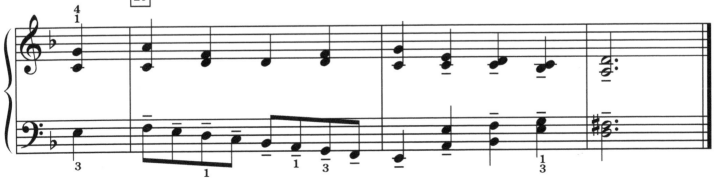

In December of 1865, Phillips Brooks, a 30-year-old minister from Philadelphia, was in the Holy Land. On Christmas Eve, he traveled on horseback to Bethlehem to visit the site where the shepherds had been when they saw the Star. Brooks was deeply moved by the experience and later wrote the words for *O Little Town of Bethlehem,* intending it as a children's hymn. He gave his poem to his church's organist, Lewis Redner, who composed the lovely melody in time for Christmas 1868.

Words only, p. 137

 # O Little Town of Bethlehem

Words by Phillips Brooks

Music by Lewis H. Redner

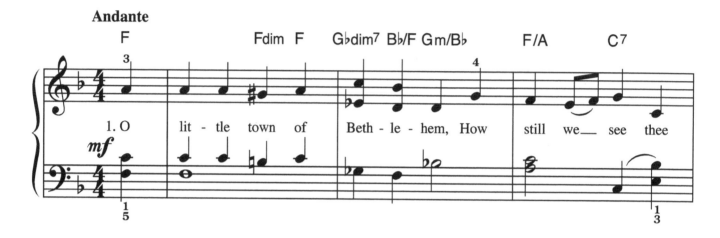

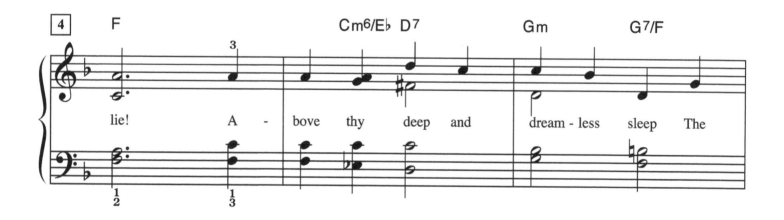

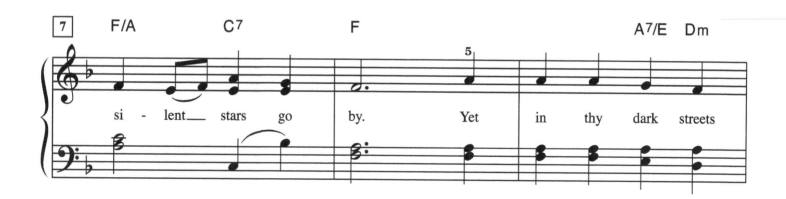

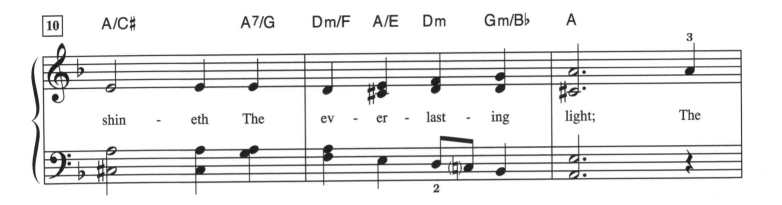

shin - eth The ev - er - last - ing light; The

hopes and fears of all the years Are met in thee to - night.

2. For Christ is born of Mary, and gathered all above,
   While mortals sleep, the angels keep their watch of wond'ring love.
   O morning stars together proclaim the holy birth!
   And praises sing to God the King and peace to men on earth.

3. How silently, how silently the wond'rous gift is giv'n!
   So God imparts to human hearts the blessings of His heav'n.
   No ear may hear His coming, but in this world of sin,
   Where meek souls will receive Him still, the dear Christ enters in.

4. Where children pure and happy pray to the blessed Child,
   Where misery cries out to Thee, Son of the mother mild;
   Where charity stands watching and faith holds wide the door,
   The dark night wakes, the glory breaks, and Christmas comes once more.

5. O holy Child of Bethlehem, descend to us we pray;
   Cast out our sin and enter in, be born in us today.
   We hear the Christmas angels the great glad tidings tell;
   O come to us, abide with us, our Lord, Immanuel.

"Call-and-response" is a common pattern in African-American church music. In this spiritual, the lead singer sings "There's a star in the East on Christmas morn," and the choir answers "Rise up, shepherd, and follow." The call-and-response pattern entered the world of jazz in the 1920s through the arrangements of Fletcher Henderson and others.

Words only, p. 137

Rise Up, Shepherd, and Follow

African-American Spiritual

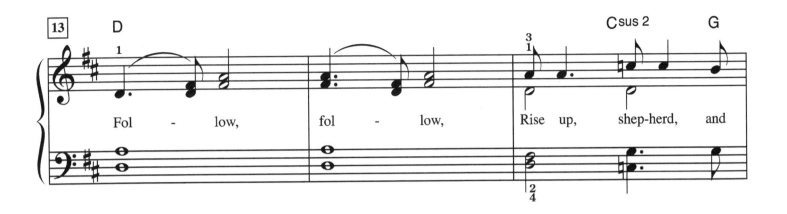

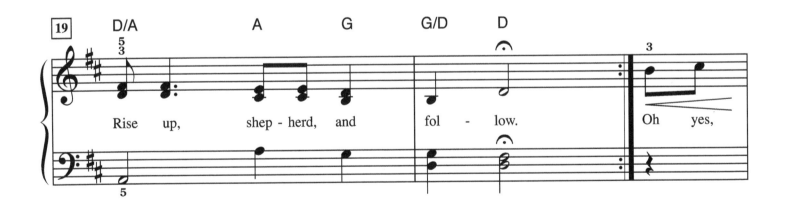

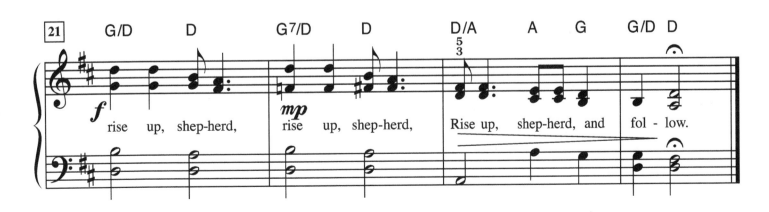

American minister John Henry Hopkins wrote this carol for a Christmas pageant in 1857. At that time, he was criticized for calling the Wise Men "kings" (the Bible only mentions "men from the East"). The three kings are: Melchior, who brings gold to crown the new King; Gaspar, who brings frankincense, an aromatic gum used to make incense; and Balthasar, whose gift of myrrh (an aromatic gum used in burials) foretells the death of Jesus on the cross.

Words only, p. 138

 # We Three Kings of Orient Are

Words and Music by
John Henry Hopkins, Jr.

2. Born a King on Bethlehem's plain,
   Gold I bring to crown Him again.
   King forever, ceasing never,
   Over us all to reign.
   (Chorus)

3. Frankincense to offer have I,
   Incense owns a Deity nigh.
   Pray'r and praising, all men raising,
   Worship Him, God most high.
   (Chorus)

4. Myrrh is mine, its bitter perfume
   Breathes a life of gathering gloom;
   Sorrowing, sighing, bleeding, dying,
   Sealed in the stone-cold tomb.
   (Chorus)

5. Glorious now behold Him arise,
   King and God and Sacrifice.
   Alleluia, Alleluia,
   Earth to heav'n replies.
   (Chorus)

This beautiful carol uses the melody of the song *Greensleeves,* a song people have been singing, playing, and dancing to for over 400 years. Originally, the piece was played rather fast for dancing, but its real beauty was not revealed until someone had the inspiration to slow it down. In 1865, insurance man and sometime poet William Chatterton Dix wrote the words to the carol we sing today.

Words only, p. 138

What Child Is This?

Words by William Chatterton Dix

16th-century English Melody
("Greensleeves")

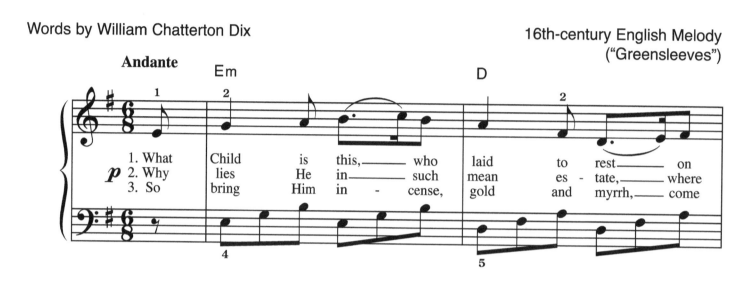

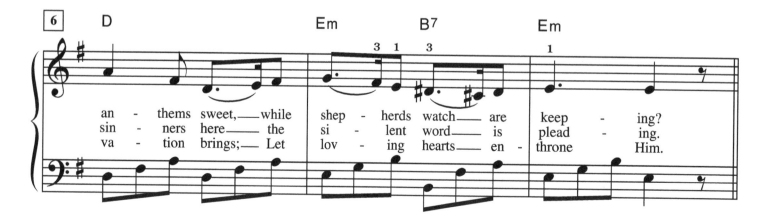

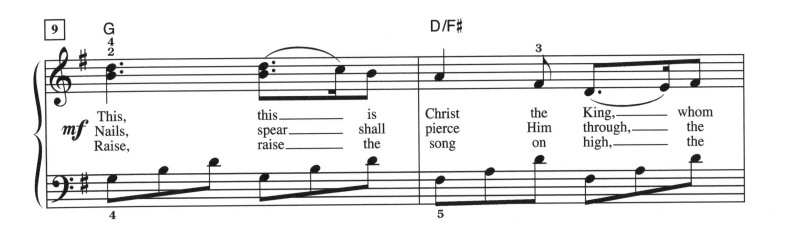

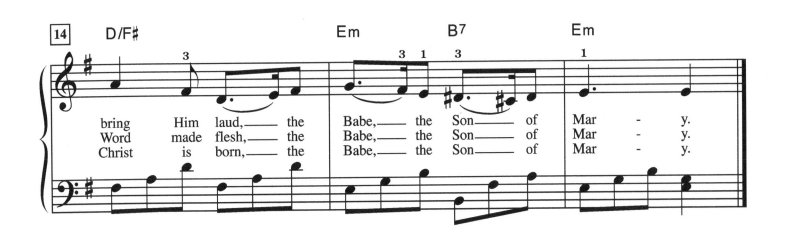

The 12 days last from Christmas Day to Epiphany on January 6. The custom of gift-giving arose from the first Epiphany, when the Wise Men brought gifts to the infant Jesus. This is a "cumulative" carol, with each verse mentioning an additional gift for each of the 12 days. Although this carol wasn't published until 1868, it was known at least 300 years earlier.

Words only, p. 138

The Twelve Days of Christmas

Traditional

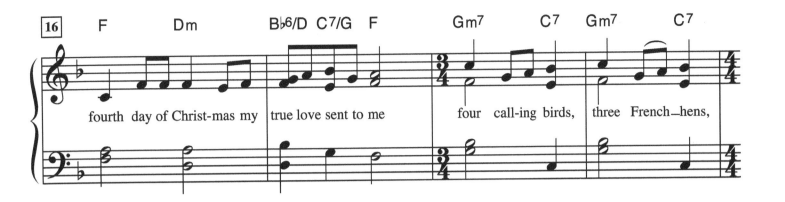

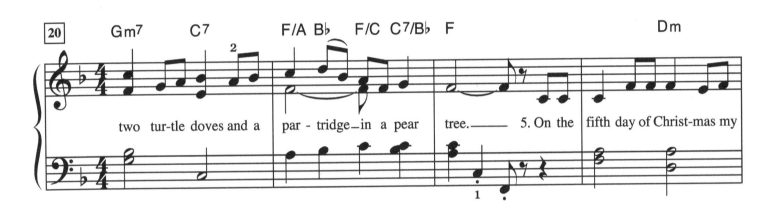

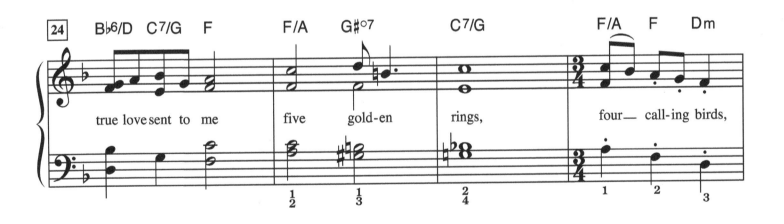

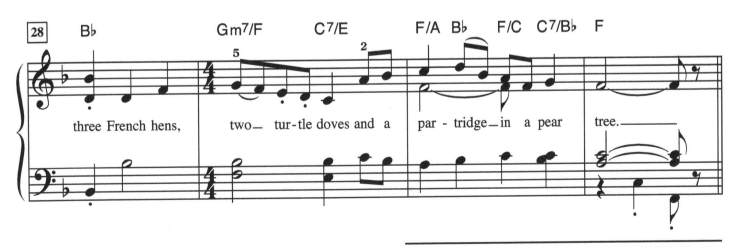

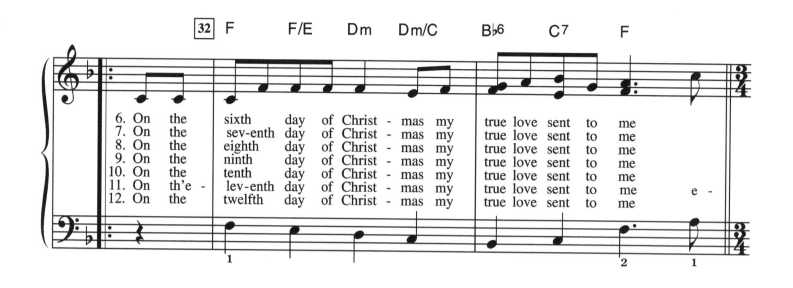

32 F   F/E   Dm   Dm/C   B♭6   C7   F

6. On the sixth day of Christ - mas my true love sent to me
7. On the sev-enth day of Christ - mas my true love sent to me
8. On the eighth day of Christ - mas my true love sent to me
9. On the ninth day of Christ - mas my true love sent to me
10. On the tenth day of Christ - mas my true love sent to me
11. On th'e - lev-enth day of Christ - mas my true love sent to me   e -
12. On the twelfth day of Christ - mas my true love sent to me

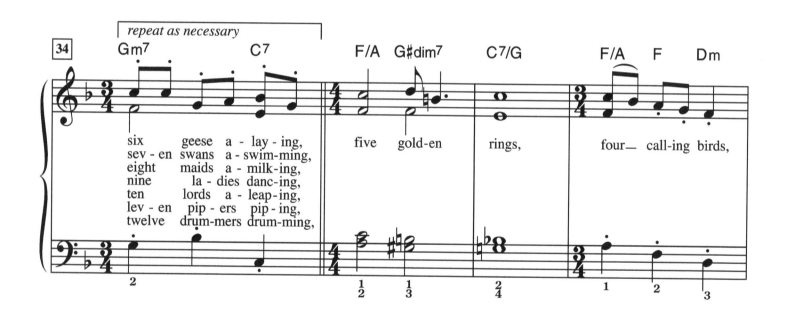

repeat as necessary

34 Gm7   C7   F/A G♯dim7   C7/G   F/A   F   Dm

six   geese a - lay-ing,   five gold-en   rings,   four— call-ing birds,
sev - en swans a - swim-ming,
eight   maids a - milk-ing,
nine   la - dies danc-ing,
ten   lords a - leap-ing,
lev - en pip - ers pip-ing,
twelve drum-mers drum-ming,

38 B♭   Gm7/F   C7/E   F/A B♭ F/C C7/B♭ F

three French hens,   two— tur-tle doves and a   par - tridge—in a pear   tree.——

The story of "Rudolph, the Red-Nosed Reindeer" was written in 1939 by Robert L. May, as a promotional piece for the Montgomery Ward department stores. May's brother-in-law, songwriter Johnny Marks, adapted the story into a song and persuaded Gene Autry to record it. Subsequently, the song has been recorded by over 500 different artists, and went on to sell almost 200 million records and 5 million copies of sheet music, making it one of the best-selling songs of all time.

Words only, p. 139

Rudolph, the Red-Nosed Reindeer

Words and Music by
Johnny Marks

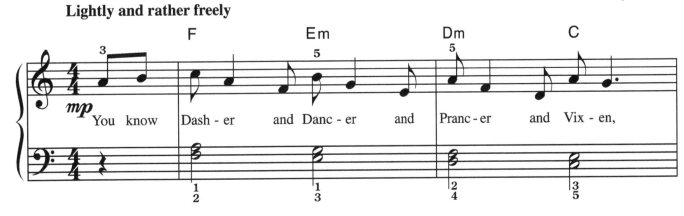

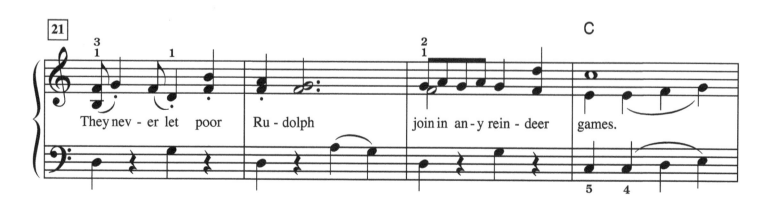

Surely one of the most popular children's Christmas songs ever written, Frosty first appeared as a story, then as a television special that featured this song. Actor/comedian Jimmy Durante made his last appearance as the narrator of this animated special. Songwriters Steve Nelson and Jack Rollins perfectly captured the fun and magic of a snowman who comes to life, even if only briefly.

Words only, p. 139

Frosty the Snowman

Words and Music by
Steve Nelson and Jack Rollins

Frost - y the Snow-man was a jol - ly, hap - py soul, With a
Frost - y the Snow-man knew the sun was hot that day, So he

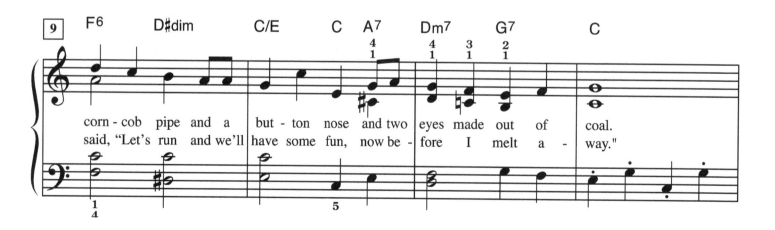

corn - cob pipe and a but - ton nose and two eyes made out of coal.
said, "Let's run and we'll have some fun, now be - fore I melt a - way."

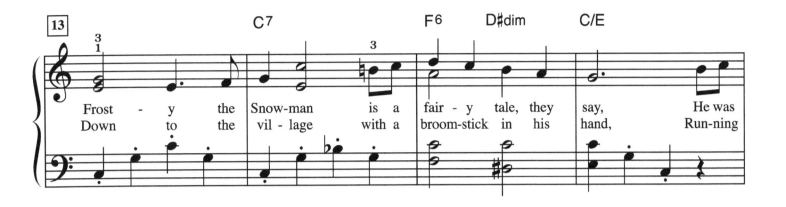

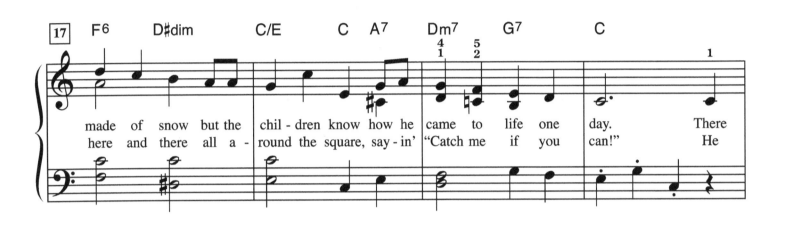

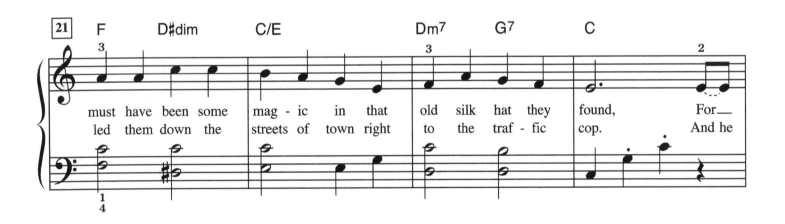

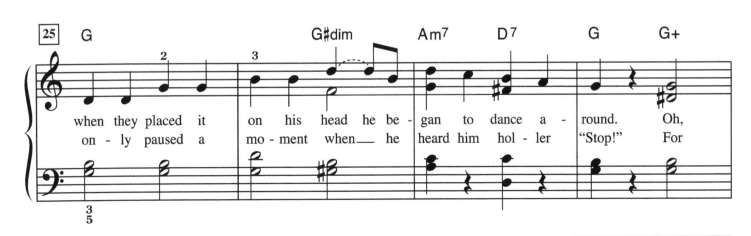

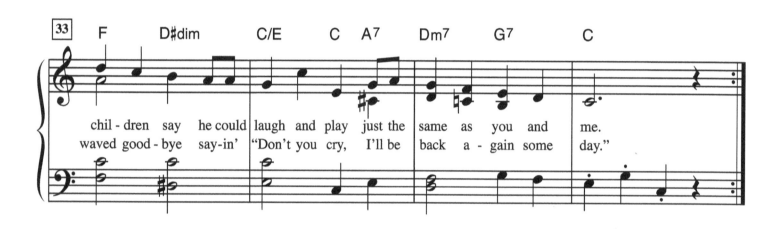

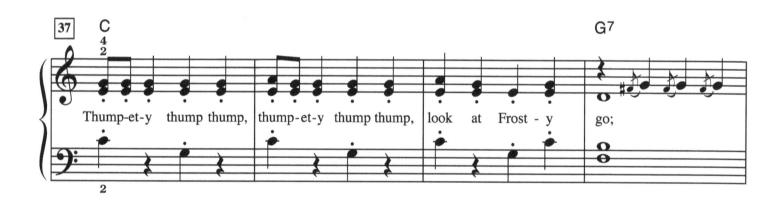

No one knows who wrote this beautiful carol. It was first published in the late 18th century in translation from a book called *Musical and Poetical Relicks of the Welsh Bards.* Since then the original poem has been modified many times, but this version is the best known.

Words only, p. 140

All Through the Night

Traditional Welsh Carol

A product of long-time collaborators Sid Tepper and Roy Bennett, this delightful children's song was dedicated to Tepper's daughter Susan. The title was also used in an animated Christmas cartoon, and for a doll that sold in the 1950s.

Words only, p. 140

Suzy Snowflake

Words and Music by
Sid Tepper and Roy C. Bennett

Victor Herbert and Glen MacDonough wrote their hit Broadway musical *Babes in Toyland,* which premiered in 1903. In 1934, a movie version featuring the comedy team of Laurel and Hardy brought the play to a much wider audience.

Words only, p. 140

Toyland

Words by Glen MacDonough

Music by Victor Herbert

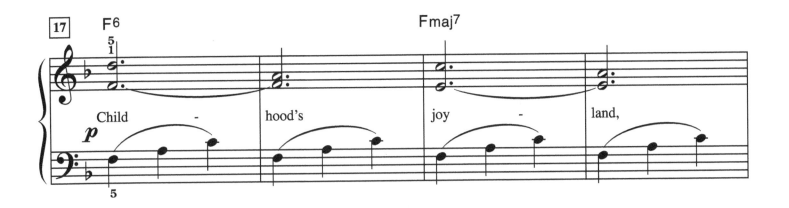

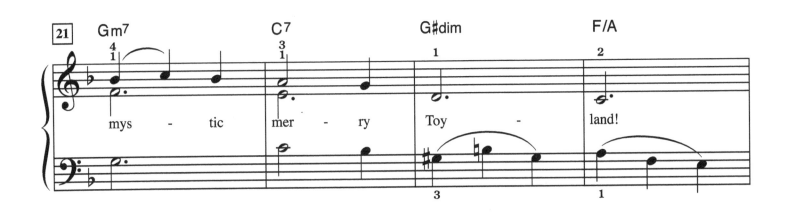

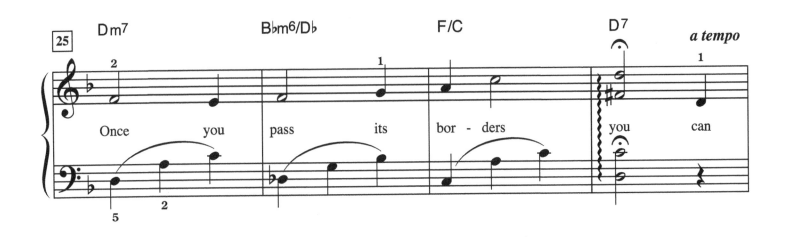

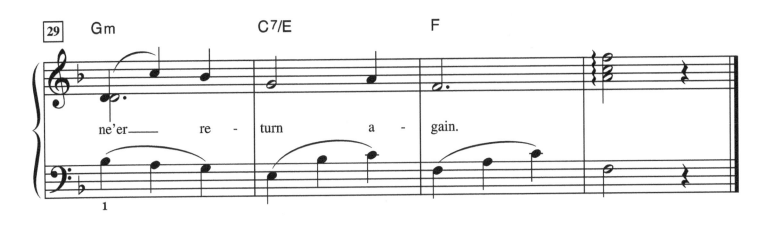

Children (and most adults) love animals. In this charming 12th-century English carol, every animal in the stable has a special task: the donkey has brought Mary to Bethlehem; the cow has given up her manger for the baby Jesus; the sheep has given its wool for a blanket; the dove coos the baby to sleep; and even the stubborn, bad-tempered camel has brought the Wise Men to worship at the baby's manger.

Words only, p. 140

The Friendly Beasts

Traditional

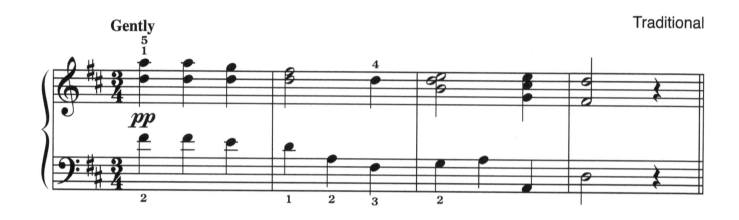

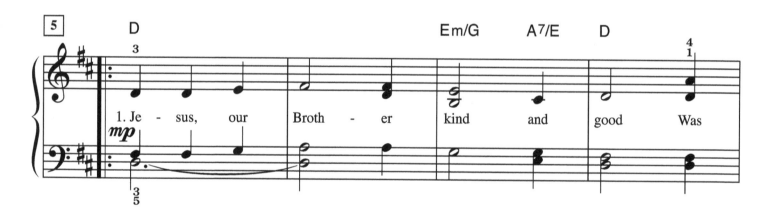

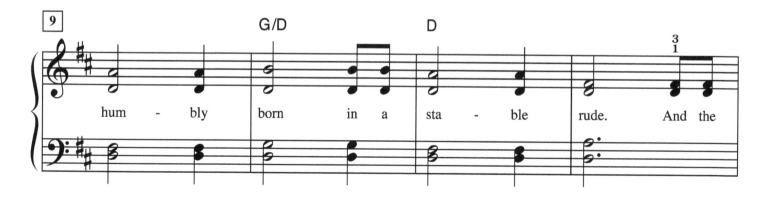

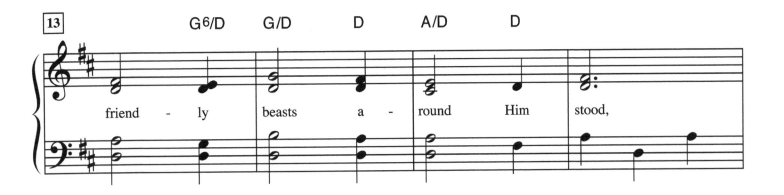

friend - ly beasts a - round Him stood,

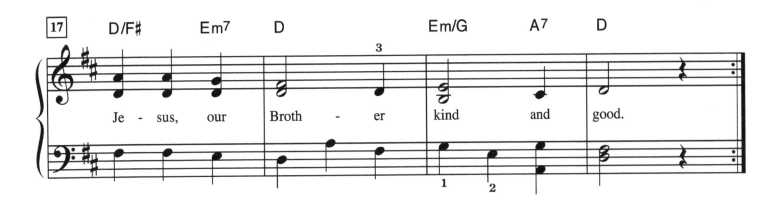

Je - sus, our Broth - er kind and good.

2. "I," said the donkey, shaggy and brown,
   "I carried His mother up hill and down;
   I carried her safely to Bethlehem town.
   I," said the donkey, shaggy and brown.

3. "I," said the cow, all white and red,
   "I gave Him my manger for a bed;
   I gave Him my hay to pillow His head.
   I," said the cow, all white and red.

4. "I," said the sheep with curly horn,
   "I gave Him my wool for His blanket warm;
   He wore my coat on Christmas morn.
   I," said the sheep with curly horn.

5. "I," said the dove from the rafters high,
   "Cooed Him to sleep that He should not cry;
   We cooed Him to sleep, my mate and I.
   I," said the dove from the rafters high.

6. "I," said the camel, yellow and black,
   "Over the desert, upon my back
   I brought Him a gift in the Wise Men's pack.
   I," said the camel, yellow and black.

7. Thus every beast by some good spell
   In the stable dark was glad to tell
   Of the gift he gave Emmanuel,
   The gift he gave Emmanuel.

James Murray first published this children's carol in his *Dainty Songs for Little Lads and Lasses* in 1887. He called it "Luther's Cradle Hymn" (supposedly composed by Martin Luther for his children). However, there is no evidence that Martin Luther had anything to do with it, and most authorities now believe that Murray himself wrote the music.

Away in a Manger

Words only, p. 140

Words: Anonymous (stanzas 1, 2)
John Thomas McFarland (stanza 3)

Music by James R. Murray

Cledus T. Judd, the country singer who recorded this comedy song said: "A couple of good friends of mine, Elmo and Patsy, wrote me and said they's written the perfect country Christmas song. I said, 'You pretty much got it all: Grandma, the family, getting drunk and run over by heavy machinery.'"

Words only, p. 141

Grandma Got Run Over by a Reindeer

Words and Music by
Randy Brooks

Moderato

Grand-ma got run o-ver by a rein-deer_____ walk-ing home from our house Christ-mas Eve.

You can say there's no such thing as

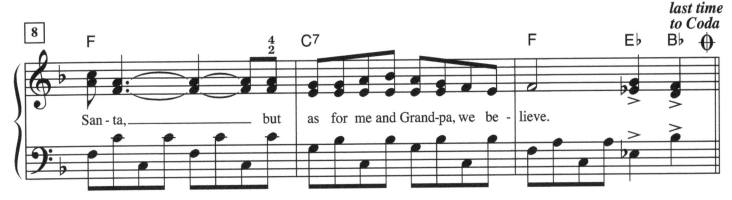

San-ta,_____ but as for me and Grand-pa, we be-lieve.

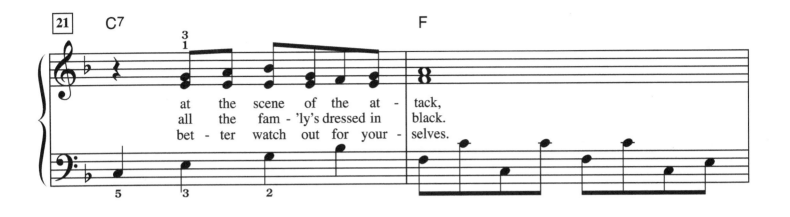

at the scene of the at - tack,
all the fam - 'ly's dressed in black.
bet - ter watch out for your - selves.

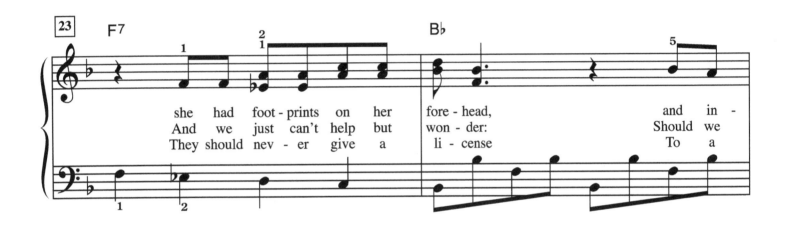

she had foot - prints on her fore - head, and in -
And we just can't help but won - der: Should we
They should nev - er give a li - cense To a

crim - i - nat - ing Claus marks on her back.
o - pen up her gifts or send them back.
man who drives a sleigh and plays with elves.

Coda

N.C.

Bandleader Spike Jones was famous for parodying dozens of "serious" songs by using gunshots, screams, squeaks, gurgles, gargles and other noises to hilarious effect. In 1948, he and his band, The City Slickers, had a big hit with this song, unforgettably sung by chubby lead trumpeter George Rock, wearing short pants with his two front teeth blacked out.

Words only, p. 141

All I Want for Christmas Is My Two Front Teeth

Words and Music by
Don Gardner

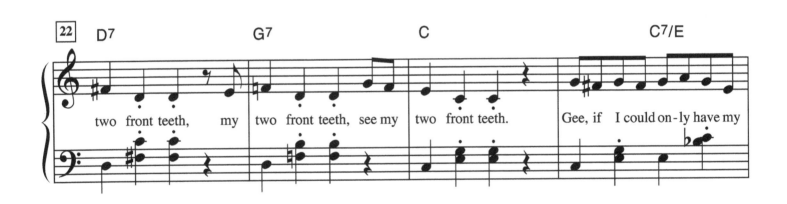

Take a story by that master of nonsense—Dr. Seuss—combine it with the talents of rubber-faced comedian Jim Carrey, add songs by Albert Hague, and what do you have? Simply one of the most charming movies ever made about Christmas, *The Grinch.* Based on Dr. Seuss' children's book, *How the Grinch Stole Christmas,* the film tells the tale of a grumpy old hermit who finds the true meaning of Christmas.

Words only, p. 141

Welcome Christmas
(from *The Grinch*)

Lyrics by Dr. Seuss

Music by Albert Hague

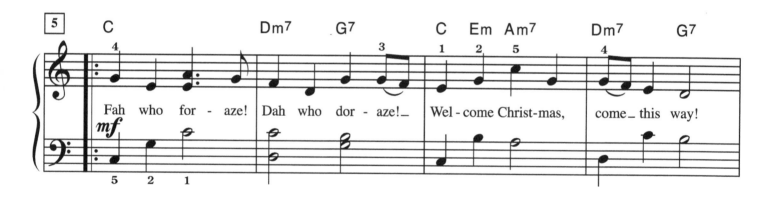

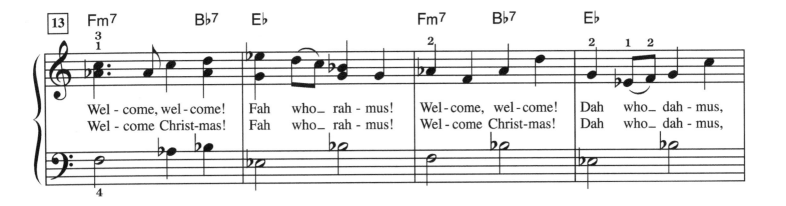

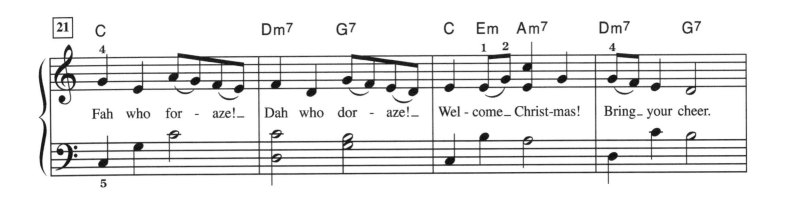

Songwriters love "laundry list" tunes—songs that enumerate a series of related things. One of writer Roy Bennett's daughters once spilled some ink on her mother's rug, and was threatened with getting "nuttin'" for Christmas. This served as the inspiration for these lyrics—a "laundry list" of naughty things a child might do—and a hit song was born.

Words only, p. 142

Nuttin' for Christmas

Words and Music by
Sid Tepper and Roy C. Bennett

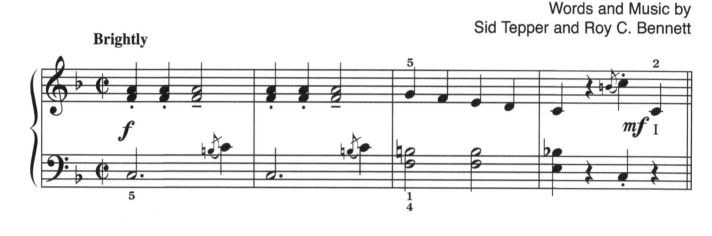

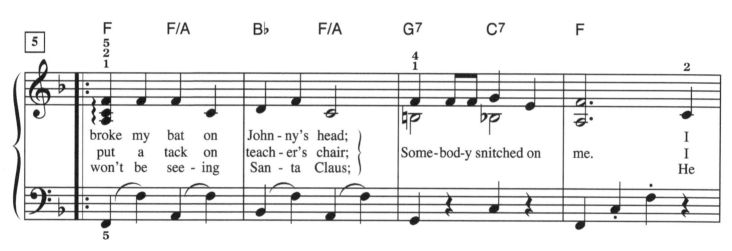

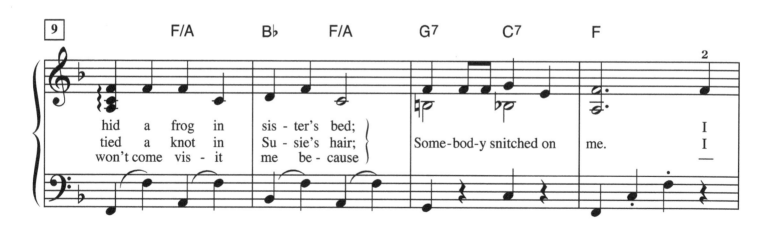

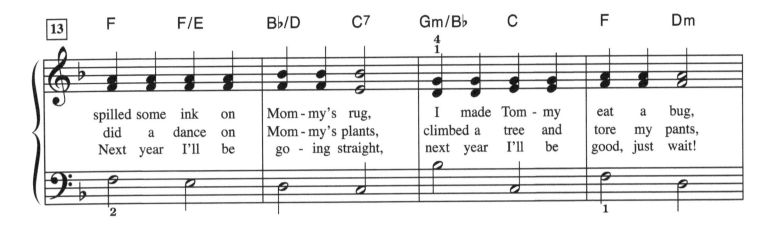

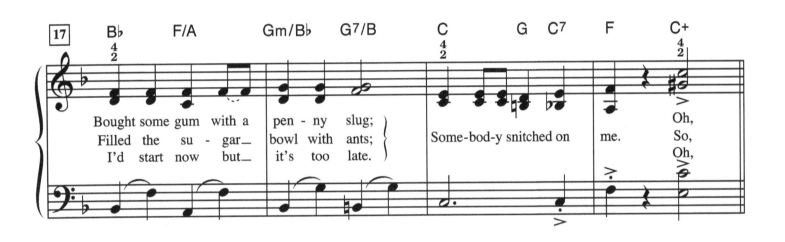

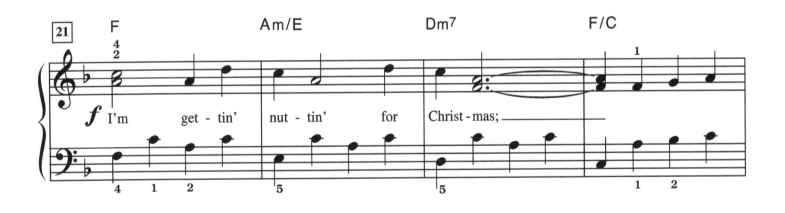

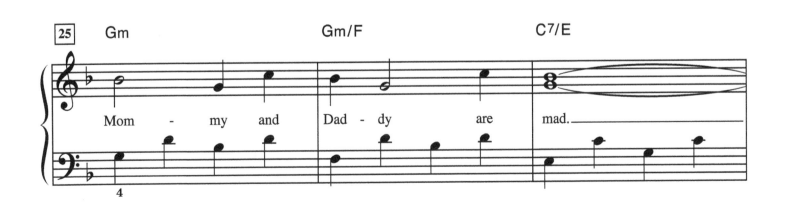

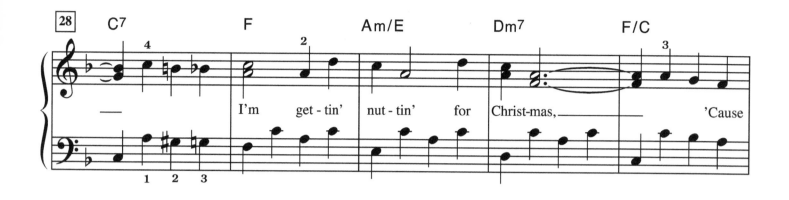

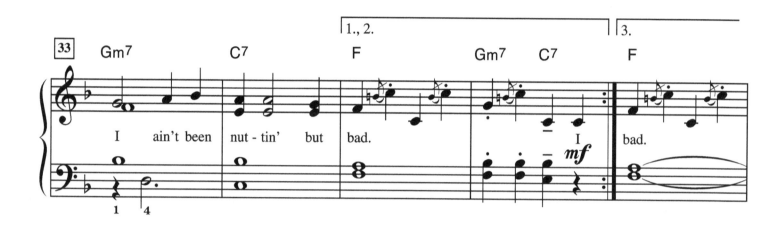

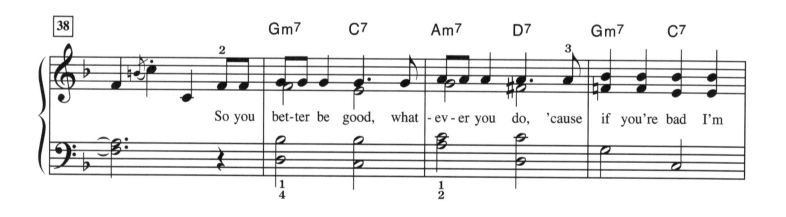

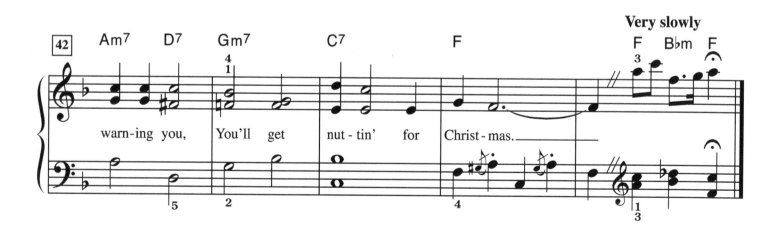

Leroy Anderson (1908–1975) was one of the finest American composers of light music in the 1900s. His best-known works include "The Syncopated Clock," "Blue Tango," "Serenata," and this spirited composition, an evocation of a New England sleigh ride. Anderson was from Massachusetts, where he studied with the great composer and educator Walter Piston, among others. The song's lyricist, Mitchell Parish, wrote many lyrics for Anderson, as well as dozens of other hits including Hoagy Carmichael's "Star Dust."

Words only, p. 142

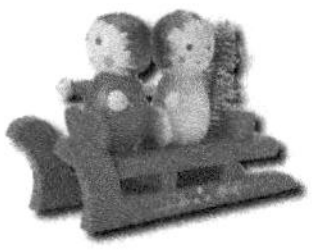

Sleigh Ride

Words by Mitchell Parish

Music by Leroy Anderson

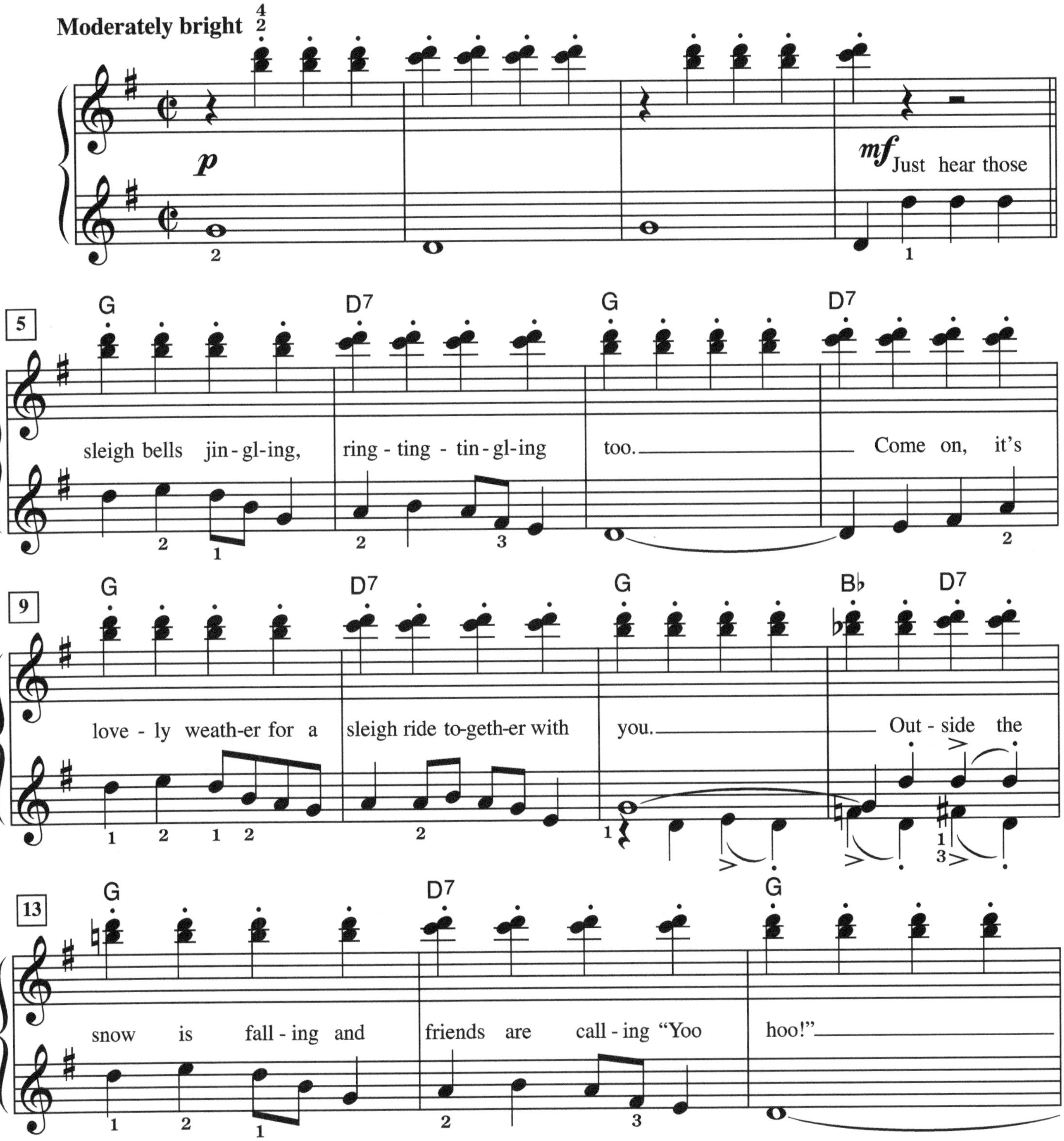

Moderately bright
p
mf Just hear those
5
G D7 G D7
sleigh bells jin - gl - ing, ring - ting - tin - gl - ing too. Come on, it's
9
G D7 G B♭ D7
love - ly weath-er for a sleigh ride to-geth-er with you. Out - side the
13
G D7 G
snow is fall - ing and friends are call - ing "Yoo hoo!"

Undoubtedly the most popular of Tchaikovsky's ballets, *The Nutcracker* is still performed in dozens, perhaps hundreds of venues throughout the world every Christmastime. Although Russian composer Peter Ilyich Tchaikovsky (1840–1893) lived an anxiety-ridden and tortured life, there's no trace of depression or sadness in the music for this ballet, a children's favorite.

Arabian Dance

(from *The Nutcracker*)

Music by
Peter Ilyich Tchaikovsky

Ukrainian composer Mykola Leontovich portrayed the sound of Christmas bells in his choral work *Shchedryk,* which was first performed in Kiev in 1916. Twenty years later, composer and conductor Peter J. Wilhousky adapted Leontovich's music and added lyrics, creating the well-loved carol that we know today. The instrumental version of the piece is included here.

The Ukrainian Bell Carol

Music by
Mykola Leontovich

Italian-born composer Pietro A. Yon (1886–1943) won many prizes for performance on piano and organ before coming to the United States in 1907. After several prestigious appointments as organist, Yon became the organist at St. Patrick's Cathedral in New York City. Among his many choral and organ works, this piece—composed in 1917—is the best known. In this work, he ingeniously combines his own melody with the traditional *Adeste Fideles*.

Gesú Bambino
(The Infant Jesus)

Words only, p. 142

Words and Music by
Pietro A. Yon

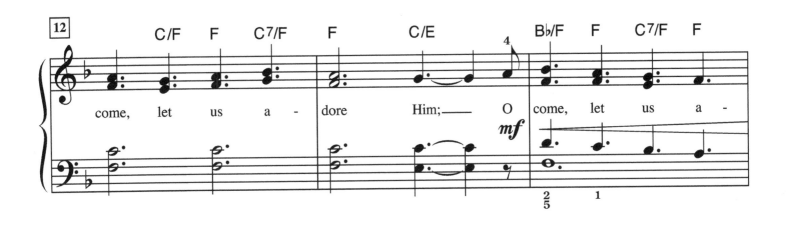

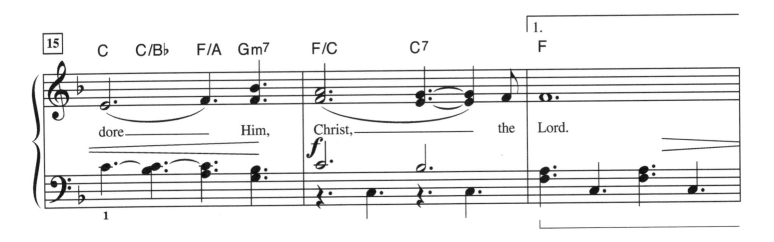

In the 19th century, Henry Wadsworth Longfellow (1807–1882) was one of America's favorite poets. His many works include *Song of Hiawatha* and a translation of Dante's *Divine Comedy*. The words to this powerful statement of faith were set to music by British pianist, organist, and composer Jean Baptiste Calkin (1827–1905). In modern times, the same words were set to music by Johnny Marks (of "Rudolph, the Red-Nosed Reindeer" fame).

Words only, p. 143

 # I Heard the Bells on Christmas Day

Words by Henry Wadsworth Longfellow

Music by Jean Baptiste Calkin

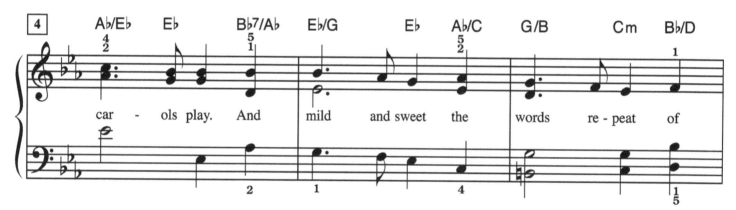

bring out the LH

2. I thought how, as the day had come,
   The belfries of all Christendom
   Had rolled along th'unbroken song
   Of peace on earth, good will to men.

3. And in despair I bow'd my head:
   "There is no peace on earth," I said,
   "For hate is strong, and mocks the song
   Of peace on earth, good will to men."

4. Then pealed the bells more loud and deep:
   "God is not dead, nor doth He sleep;
   The wrong shall fail, the right prevail,
   With peace on earth, good will to men."

5. Till, ringing, singing on its way,
   The world revolved from night to day,
   A voice, a chime, a chant sublime,
   Of peace on earth, good will to men!

Since young Adolphe Charles Adam wanted to be a composer—against his father's wishes—Adolphe studied music in secret. When his father found out, he recognized the boy's talent and relented on the condition that he never write for the stage. After Adolphe had become France's most famous composer of comic operas, his father finally forgave him. Today, Adolphe Charles Adam is chiefly remembered for his charming ballet *Giselle,* and *Cantique de Noël,* which we call "O Holy Night." The English words were written by Boston music critic and teacher John Sullivan Dwight (1818–1893).

Words only, p. 143

O Holy Night
(Cantique de Noël)

Words by Placide Cappeau
English translation by John Sullivan Dwight

Music by Adolphe Charles Adam

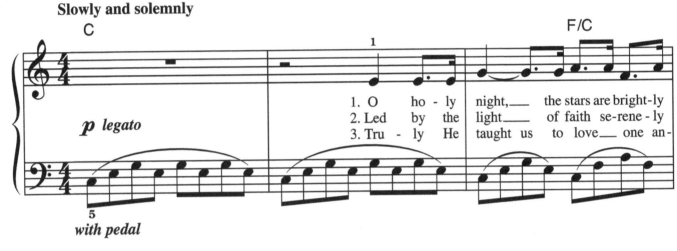

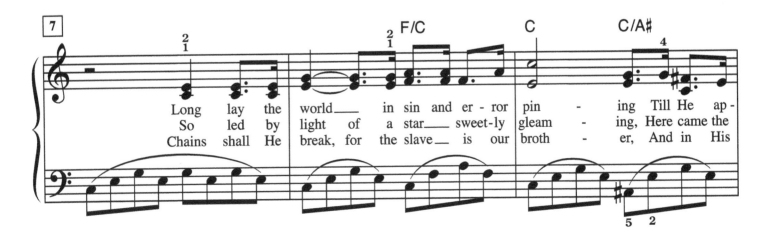

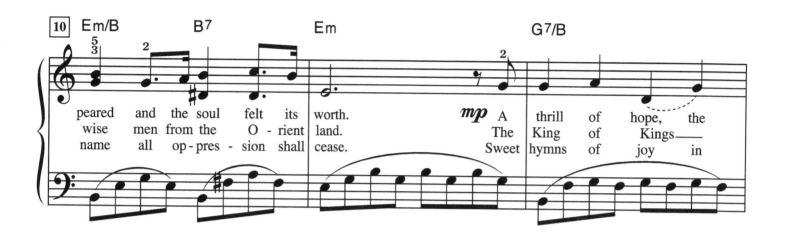

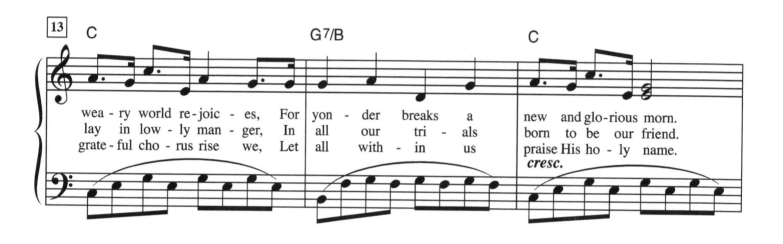

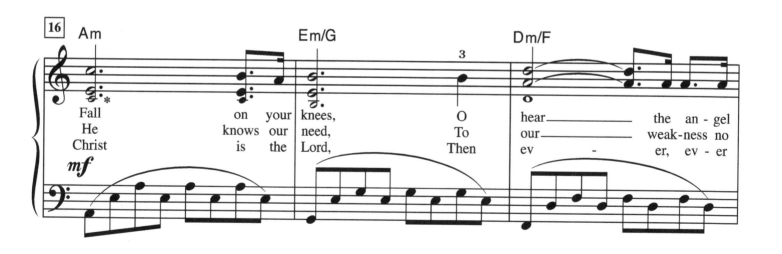

*Players who can reach may add the smaller notes.

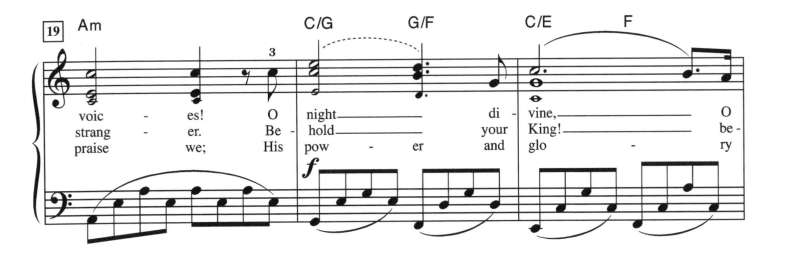

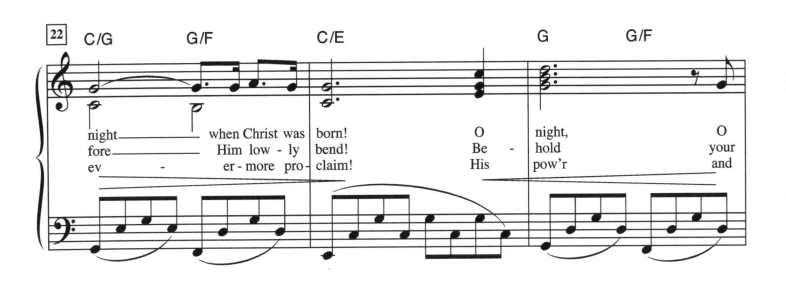

Rock and roll was in its first bloom as a new type of American music when songwriter Johnny Marks (who already had phenomenal success with "Rudolph the Red-Nosed Reindeer") contributed this effort from his prolific pen in 1958. Songstress Brenda Lee made the tune famous with her successful recording of the song.

Words only, p. 143

Rockin' Around the Christmas Tree

Words and Music by
Johnny Marks

Back in the mid-50s, rock and roll was starting to dominate record sales and airplay… so it's no wonder that the Christmas season would soon be "invaded" as well. Amateur songwriters Joe Beal and Jim Boothe hit it big with this Christmas song in a best-selling record by Bobby Helms, which is still played every Christmas a half century later!

Words only, p. 144

Jingle Bell Rock

Words and Music by
Joe Beal and Jim Boothe

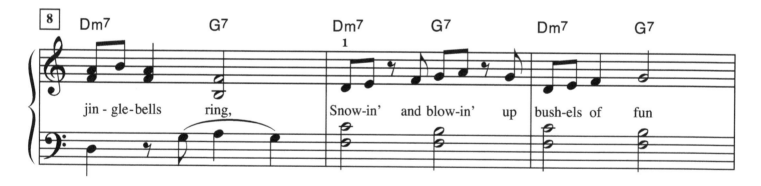

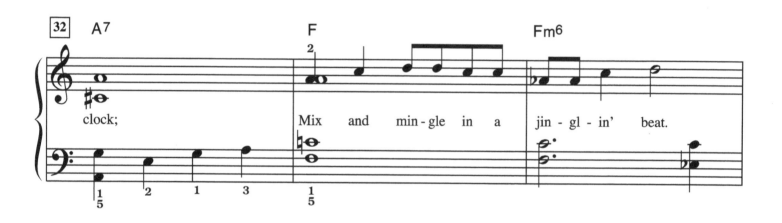

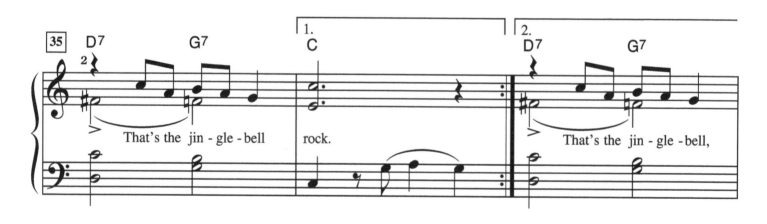

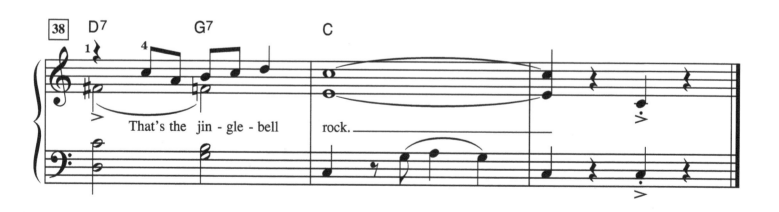

By the end of the 1920s, most American families had access to a radio, which became the focus of family evenings at home. At midnight on the last day of 1929, the popular orchestra of Guy Lombardo and His Royal Canadians broadcast their tremulous version of "Auld Lang Syne." Since then, the song has been obligatory on New Year's Eve. Strangely, little is known about its origins. The Scottish poet Robert Burns is given credit for some of the verses, but the first and best-known verse, as well as the music, are of unknown authorship. The title means "old times' sake."

Words only, p. 144

Auld Lang Syne

Words by Robert Burns

Music: Traditional Scottish Melody

In the late 1830s, England established a reliable, inexpensive postal service, which encouraged the writing of letters and cards, especially Christmas cards. The colorful cards often showed scenes of carolers, called *waits,* strolling snowy streets and singing for a bit of pudding or a cup of good cheer. This famous Christmas song was originally a waits carol, which became popular in mid-19th century England.

Words only, p. 144

 # We Wish You a Merry Christmas

Traditional

Brightly, with spirit

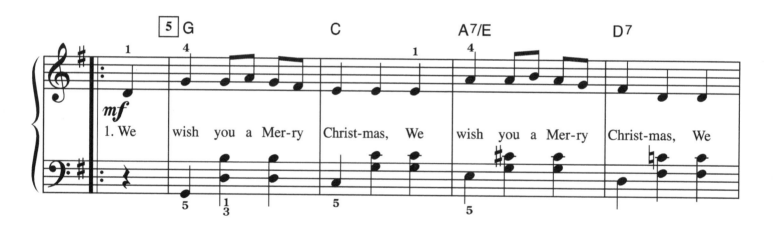

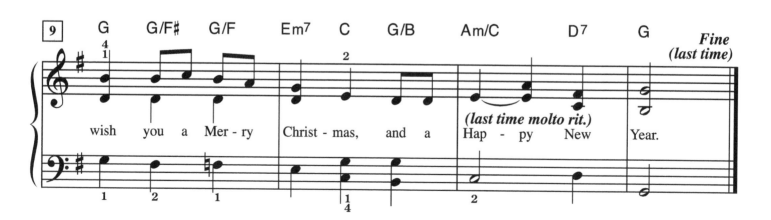

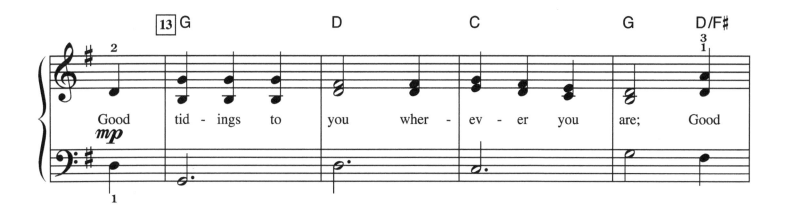

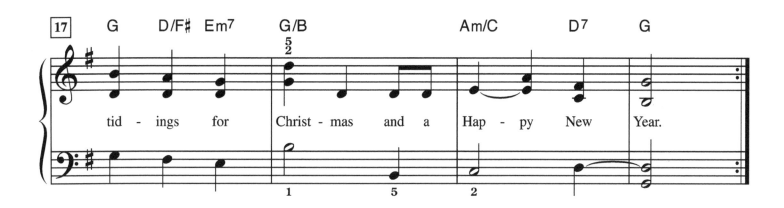

2. Oh, bring us a figgy pudding,
   Oh, bring us a figgy pudding,
   Oh, bring us a figgy pudding,
   And a cup of good cheer.
   Good tidings to you wherever you are;
   Good tidings for Christmas
   and a Happy New Year.

3. We won't go until we've got some,
   We won't go until we've got some,
   We won't go until we've got some,
   So bring some out here.
   Good tidings to you wherever you are,
   Good tidings for Christmas
   and a Happy New Year.

4. We wish you a Merry Christmas,
   We wish you a Merry Christmas,
   We wish you a Merry Christmas,
   and a Happy New Year.

Alphabetical Index

BEST POPULAR SONGS ABOUT CHRISTMAS

THE CHRISTMAS SONG 4

(Chestnuts Roasting on an Open Fire)
Lyric and Music by
Mel Tormé and Robert Wells

Although it's been said many times, many ways,
"Merry Christmas to you."
Chestnuts roasting on an open fire,
Jack Frost nipping at your nose,
Yuletide carols being sung by a choir
And folks dressed up like Eskimos.
Ev'rybody knows a turkey and some mistletoe
Help to make the season bright.
Tiny tots with their eyes all aglow
Will find it hard to sleep tonight.
They know that Santa's on his way,
He's loaded lots of toys and goodies on his sleigh.
And ev'ry mother's child is gonna spy
To see if reindeer really know how to fly.
And so I'm offering this simple phrase
To kids from one to ninety-two:
Although it's been said many times, many ways,
"Merry Christmas to you."

C-H-R-I-S-T-M-A-S 8

Words and Music by
Eddy Arnold and Jenny Lou Carson

"C" is for the Christ child born upon this day;
"H" for herald angels in the night.
"R" means our Redeemer;
"I" means Israel;
"S" is for the star that shone so bright.
"T" is for three wise men, they who traveled far.
"M" is for the manger where He lay.
"A"'s for all He stands for;
"S" means shepherds came,
And that's why there's a Christmas Day.

WINTER WONDERLAND 10

Words by Dick Smith
Music by Felix Bernard

Sleigh bells ring, are you list'nin'?
In the lane snow is glist'nin',
A beautiful sight, we're happy tonight,
Walkin' in a winter wonderland.
Gone away is the bluebird,

Here to stay is a new bird,
He sings a love song as we go along,
Walkin' in a winter wonderland.

In the meadow we can build a snowman
Then pretend that he is Parson Brown;
He'll say, "Are you married?" We'll say, "No, man!
But you can do the job when you're in town."
Later on, we'll conspire as we dream by the fire,
To face unafraid the plans that we made,
Walkin' in a winter wonderland.

Sleigh bells ring, are you list'nin'?
In the lane snow is glist'nin',
A beautiful sight, we're happy tonight,
Walkin' in a winter wonderland.
Gone away is the bluebird,
Here to stay is a new bird,
He's singing a song as we go along,
Walkin' in a winter wonderland.

In the meadow we can build a snowman
And pretend that he's a circus clown;
We'll have lots of fun with Mister Snowman
Until the other kiddies knock 'im down!
When it snows ain't it thrillin'
Tho' your nose gets a chillin',
We'll frolic and play the Eskimo way,
Walkin' in a winter wonderland.

SANTA CLAUS IS COMIN' TO TOWN 12

Words by Haven Gillespie
Music by J. Fred Coots

You better watch out, you better not cry,
Better not pout, I'm telling you why:
Santa Claus is comin' to town.
He's making a list and checking it twice,
Gonna find out who's naughty and nice,
Santa Claus is comin' to town.

He sees you when you're sleepin',
He knows when you're awake,
He knows if you've been bad or good,
So be good for goodness sake.

Oh! You better watch out, you better not cry,
Better not pout, I'm telling you why:
Santa Claus is comin' to town.

HAVE YOURSELF A MERRY LITTLE CHRISTMAS 14

*Words and Music by
Hugh Martin and Ralph Blane*

Have yourself a merry little Christmas,
Let your heart be light,
From now on our troubles will be out of sight.
Have yourself a merry little Christmas,
Make the Yuletide gay,
From now on our troubles will be far away.

Here we are as in olden days,
Happy golden days of yore.
Faithful friends who are dear to us
Gather near to us once more.

Through the years we all will be together
If the fates allow,
Hang a shining star upon the highest bough,
And have yourself a merry little Christmas now.

LET IT SNOW! LET IT SNOW! LET IT SNOW! 16

*Words by Sammy Cahn
Music by Jule Styne*

Oh! The weather outside is frightful,
But the fire is so delightful,
And since we've no place to go:
Let it snow! Let it snow! Let it snow!

It doesn't show signs of stopping
And I brought some corn for popping;
The lights are turned way down low:
Let it snow! Let it snow! Let it snow!

When we finally kiss goodnight,
How I'll hate going out in the storm.
But if you'll really hold me tight,
All the way home I'll be warm.

The fire is slowly dying,
And, my dear, we're still goodbying,
But as long as you love me so,
Let it snow! Let it snow! Let it snow!

I'LL BE HOME FOR CHRISTMAS 18

*Lyrics by Kim Gannon
Music by Walter Kent*

I'll be home for Christmas,
You can count on me.
Please have snow and mistletoe
And presents on the tree.
Christmas Eve will find me
Where the lovelight gleams.
I'll be home for Christmas
If only in my dreams.

THE LITTLE DRUMMER BOY 20

*Words and Music by
Katherine Davis, Henry Onorati and Harry Simeone*

1. Come, they told me, pa rum pum pum pum,
   Our newborn King to see, pa rum pum pum pum,
   Our finest gifts we bring, pa rum pum pum pum,
   To lay before the King, pa rum pum pum pum,
   Rum pum pum pum, rum pum pum pum,
   So to honor Him, pa rum pum pum pum,
   When we come.

2. Baby Jesus, pa rum pum pum pum,
   I am a poor boy too, pa rum pum pum pum,
   I have no gift to bring, pa rum pum pum pum,
   That's fit to give our King, pa rum pum pum pum,
   Rum pum pum pum, rum pum pum pum,
   Shall I play for You, pa rum pum pum pum,
   On my drum?

3. Mary nodded, pa rum pum pum pum,
   The ox and lamb kept time, pa rum pum pum pum,
   I played my drum for Him, pa rum pum pum pum,
   I played my best for Him, pa rum pum pum pum,
   Rum pum pum pum, rum pum pum pum,
   Then he smiled at me, pa rum pum pum pum,
   Me and my drum.

A HOLLY JOLLY CHRISTMAS 22

Words and Music by
Johnny Marks

Have a holly jolly Christmas,
It's the best time of the year.
I don't know if there'll be snow,
But have a cup of cheer.
Have a holly jolly Christmas,
And when you walk down the street
Say hello to friends you know,
And ev'ryone you meet.

Oh, ho, the mistletoe, hung where you can see.
Somebody waits for you; kiss her once for me!
Have a holly jolly Christmas,
And in case you didn't hear:
Oh, by golly, have a holly jolly Christmas this year.

THE MERRY CHRISTMAS POLKA 24

Words and Music by
Sonny Burke and Paul Webster

They're tuning up the fiddles now,
The fiddles now, the fiddles now;
There's wine to warm the middles now
And set your head awhirl.
Around and 'round the room we go,
The room we go, the room we go;
Around and 'round the room we go,
So get yourself a girl.

Now ev'ry heart will start to tingle,
When sleigh bells jingle on Santa's sleigh;
Together we will greet Kris Kringle
And another Christmas Day.

Come on and dance The Merry Christmas Polka;
Let ev'ryone be happy and gay.
Oh, it's the time to be jolly
And deck the halls with holly
So let's have a jolly holiday.

Come on and dance The Merry Christmas Polka;
Let ev'ry lady step with her beau.
Around a tree to the ceiling
With lots of time for stealing
Those kisses beneath the mistletoe.

Come on and dance The Merry Christmas Polka;
Another joyous season has begun.
Roll out the Yuletide barrels
And sing out the carols,
A Merry Christmas ev'ryone.

Come on and dance The Merry Christmas Polka;
With ev'rybody joining in the fun.
Roll out the barrels that cheer you
And shout till they hear you,
A Merry Christmas ev'ryone.

THERE IS NO CHRISTMAS LIKE A HOME CHRISTMAS 28

Words by Carl Sigman
Music by Mickey J. Addy

There is no Christmas like a home Christmas,
With your Dad and Mother, Sis and Brother there.
With their hearts humming at your homecoming,
And that merry Yuletide spirit in the air.

Christmas bells, Christmas bells,
Ringing loud and strong;
Follow them, follow them,
You've been away too long.
There is no Christmas like a home Christmas,
For that's the time of year all roads lead home.

A MARSHMALLOW WORLD 30

Words by Carl Sigmund
Music by Peter De Rose

It's a marshmallow world in the winter
When the snow comes to cover the ground.
It's the time for play; it's a whipped-cream day;
I wait for it the whole year round.
Those are marshmallow clouds being friendly
In the arms of the evergreen tree,
And the sun is red like a pumpkin head;
It's shining so your nose won't freeze.
The world is your snowball, see how it grows;
That's how it goes whenever it snows.
The world is your snowball just for a song.
Get out and roll it along.
It's a yum-yummy world made for sweethearts,
Take a walk with your favorite girl.
It's a sugar date, what if spring is late,
In winter, it's a marshmallow world.

The Christmas Waltz 32

Words by Sammy Cahn
Music by Jule Styne

Frosted windowpanes, candles gleaming inside,
Painted candycanes on the tree;
Santa's on his way, he's filled his sleigh with things,
Things for you and for me.

It's that time of year, when the world falls in love,
Ev'ry song you hear seems to say:
"Merry Christmas, may your
New Year dreams come true."
And this song of mine in three quarter time
Wishes you and yours the same thing, too.

Christmas in Killarney 34

Words and Music by
John Redmond, James Cavanaugh and Frank Weldon

The holly green, the ivy green,
The prettiest picture you've ever seen
Is Christmas in Killarney
With all of the folks at home.
It's nice, you know, to kiss your beau
While cuddling under the mistletoe,
And Santa Claus, you know of course,
Is one of the boys from home.

The door is always open,
The neighbors pay a call.
And Father John before he's gone
Will bless the house and all.
How grand it feels to kick your heels
And join in the fun of the jigs and reels;
I'm handing you no blarney,
The likes you've never known
Is Christmas in Killarney
With all of the folks at home.

It's the Most Wonderful Time of the Year 36

Words and Music by
Eddie Pola and George Wylie

It's the most wonderful time of the year.
With the kids jingle-belling and everyone telling you,
"Be of good cheer!"
It's the most wonderful time of the year.

It's the most wonderful time of the year.
It's the hap-happiest season of all.
With those holiday greetings, and gay happy meetings
When friends come to call,
It's the hap-happiest season of all.

There'll be parties for hosting,
Marshmallows for toasting,
And caroling out in the snow.
There'll be scary ghost stories
And tales of the glories
Of Christmases long, long ago.

It's the most wonderful time of the year.
There'll be much mistletoeing
And hearts will be glowing
When loved ones are near.
It's the most wonderful time of the year.

FAVORITE HYMNS, CAROLS AND SONGS ABOUT CHRISTMAS

Words by Joseph Mohr
Music by Franz Gruber

1. Silent night, holy night,
   All is calm, all is bright
   'Round yon Virgin Mother and Child,
   Holy Infant so tender and mild,
   Sleep in heavenly peace,
   Sleep in heavenly peace.

2. Silent night, holy night,
   Shepherds quake at the sight.
   Glories stream from heaven afar,
   Heav'nly hosts sing Alleluia;
   Christ, the Savior is born;
   Christ, the Savior is born.

3. Silent night, holy night,
   Son of God, love's pure light;
   Radiant beams from Thy holy face,
   With the dawn of redeeming grace,
   Jesus, Lord, at Thy birth;
   Jesus, Lord, at Thy birth.

Words and Music by
James Pierpont

Dashing through the snow
In a one-horse open sleigh,
O'er the fields we go,
Laughing all the way.
Bells on bob-tail ring,
Making spirits bright;
What fun it is to laugh and sing
A sleighing song tonight. Oh!

Jingle bells, jingle bells, jingle all the way.
Oh, what fun it is to ride in a one-horse open sleigh.
Jingle bells, jingle bells, jingle all the way.
Oh, what fun it is to ride in a one-horse open sleigh.

Traditional

1. Angels we have heard on high,
   Sweetly singing o'er the plains,
   And the mountains in reply
   Echoing their joyous strains.
   Gloria in excelsis Deo,
   Gloria in excelsis Deo.

2. Shepherds, why this jubilee?
   Why your joyous strains prolong?
   What the gladsome tidings be
   Which inspire your heav'nly song?
   Gloria in excelsis Deo,
   Gloria in excelsis Deo.

3. Come to Bethlehem and see
   Him Whose birth the angels sing.
   Come adore on bended knee
   Christ the Lord, the newborn King.
   Gloria in excelsis Deo,
   Gloria in excelsis Deo.

Traditional Welsh Carol

1. Deck the hall with boughs of holly,
   Fa la la la la la la la la.
   'Tis the season to be jolly,
   Fa la la la la la la la la.
   Don we now our gay apparel,
   Fa la, fa la, la la la.
   Troll the ancient Yuletide carol,
   Fa la la la la la la la la.

2. See the blazing Yule before us,
   Fa la la la la la la la la.
   Strike the harp and join the chorus,
   Fa la la la la la la la la.
   Follow me in merry measure,
   Fa la, fa la, la la la.
   While I tell of Yuletide treasure,
   Fa la la la la la la la la.

3. Fast away the old year passes,
   Fa la la la la la la la la.
   Hail the new, ye lads and lasses,
   Fa la la la la la la la la.
   Sing we joyous all together,
   Fa la, fa la, la la la.
   Heedless of the wind and weather,
   Fa la la la la la la la la.

African-American Spiritual

1. When I was a sinner
   I prayed both night and day;
   I asked the Lord to aid me,
   And He showed me the way.

Go, tell it on the mountain,
Over the hills and ev'rywhere;
Go, tell it on the mountain:
Our Jesus Christ is born.

2. When I was a seeker
   I sought both night and day;
   I asked the Lord to help me,
   And He taught me how to pray.

(Chorus)

3. Down in a lowly manger
   The humble Christ was born;
   And God sent us salvation
   That blessed Christmas morn.

(Chorus)

THE FIRST NOEL 46
Traditional

1. The first Noel, the angels did say,
   Was to certain poor shepherds in fields as they
   lay;
   In fields where they lay keeping their sheep,
   On a cold winter's night that was so deep.

Noel, Noel, Noel, Noel,
Born is the King of Israel.

2. They lookéd up and saw a star,
   Shining in the East beyond them far;
   And to the earth it gave great light,
   And so it continued day and night.

(Chorus)

3. This star drew nigh to the northwest;
   O'er Bethlehem it took its rest,
   And there it did both stop and stay,
   Right o'er the place where Jesus lay.

(Chorus)

4. Then entered in those Wise Men three,
   Full rev'rently upon their knee,
   And offered there in His presence
   Their gold and myrrh and frankincense.

(Chorus)

GOD REST YE MERRY, GENTLEMEN 48
Traditional

1. God rest ye merry, gentlemen,
   Let nothing you dismay.
   Remember Christ our Savior
   Was born on Christmas Day;
   To save us all from Satan's pow'r
   When we were gone astray.

O tidings of comfort and joy, comfort and joy,
O tidings of comfort and joy.

2. In Bethlehem in Jewry
   This blesséd Babe was born,
   And laid within a manger
   Upon this blesséd morn;
   To which His mother Mary
   Did nothing take in scorn.

(Chorus)

3. From God our heavenly Father
   A blesséd angel came,
   And unto certain shepherds
   Brought tidings of the same,
   How that in Bethlehem was born
   The Son of God by name.

(Chorus)

4. "Fear not," then said the angel,
   "Let nothing you affright;
   This day was born a Savior
   Of a pure Virgin bright
   To free all those who trust in Him
   From Satan's power and might."

(Chorus)

5. The shepherds at those tidings
   Rejoicéd much in mind
   And left their flocks a-feeding
   In tempest, storm and wind,
   And went to Bethlehem straightaway
   This blesséd Babe to find.

(Chorus)

6. But when to Bethlehem they came
   Where at this Infant lay,
   They found Him in a manger
   Where oxen feed on hay;
   His Mother Mary kneeling
   Unto the Lord did pray.

(Chorus)

7. Now to the Lord sing praises,
   All you within this place,
   And with true love and brotherhood
   Each other now embrace;
   This holy tide of Christmas
   All others doth deface.

(Chorus)

GOOD KING WENCESLAS 50

Traditional

1. Good King Wenceslas looked out
   On the Feast of Stephen,
   When the snow lay round about,
   Deep and crisp and even.
   Brightly shone the moon that night,
   Though the frost was cruel,
   When a poor man came in sight
   Gath'ring winter fuel.

2. "Hither, page, and stand by me,
   If thou know'st it, telling,
   Yonder peasant, who is he?
   Where and what his dwelling?"
   "Sire, he lives a good league hence
   Underneath the mountain,
   Right against the forest fence,
   By Saint Agnes' fountain."

3. "Bring me flesh and bring me wine,
   Bring me pine logs hither:
   Thou and I will see him dine
   When we bear them thither."
   Page and monarch, forth they went,
   Forth they went together
   Through the rude wind's wild lament
   And the bitter weather.

4. "Sire, the night is darker now
   And the wind blows stronger;
   Fails my heart, I know not how
   I can go no longer."
   "Mark my footsteps, good my page,
   Tread thou in them boldly;
   Thou shalt find the winter's rage
   Freeze thy blood less coldly."

5. In his master's steps he trod
   Where the snow lay dinted;
   Heat was in the very sod
   Which the Saint had printed.
   Therefore, Christian men be sure
   Wealth or rank possessing,
   Ye who now will bless the poor
   Shall yourselves find blessing.

HARK! THE HERALD ANGELS SING 52

Words by Charles Wesley
Music by Felix Mendelssohn

1. Hark! The herald angels sing,
   "Glory to the new-born King;
   Peace on earth, and mercy mild;
   God and sinners reconciled."
   Joyful, all ye nations rise,
   Join the triumph of the skies;
   With th'angelic host proclaim,
   "Christ is born in Bethlehem."
   Hark! The herald angels sing,
   "Glory to the newborn King."

2. Christ, by highest heav'n adored,
   Christ the everlasting Lord,
   Late in time behold Him come,
   Offspring of the Virgin's womb!
   Veiled in flesh the Godhead see;
   Hail th'incarnate Deity!
   Pleased as Man with men to dwell,
   Jesus, our Immanuel,
   Hark! The herald angels sing,
   "Glory to the newborn King."

3. Hail the heav'n-born Prince of Peace!
   Hail the Sun of Righteousness!
   Light and life to all He brings,
   Ris'n with healing in His wings.
   Mild He lays His glory by,
   Born that man no more may die,
   Born to raise the sons of earth,
   Born to give them second birth.
   Hark! The herald angels sing,
   "Glory to the newborn King."

HERE WE COME A-CAROLING 54

(The Wassail Song)
Traditional

1. Here we come a-caroling
   Among the leaves so green;
   Here we come a-wand'ring
   So fair to be seen.

Love and joy come to you,
And to you glad Christmas too,
And God bless you and send you
A Happy New Year,
And God send you a Happy New Year.

2. We are not daily beggars
   That beg from door to door,
   But we are neighbors' children
   Whom you have seen before.

(Chorus)

3. God bless the master of this house,
   Likewise the mistress too,
   And all the little children
   That 'round the table go.

(Chorus)

I SAW THREE SHIPS 56

Traditional

1. I saw three ships come sailing in
   On Christmas Day, on Christmas Day.
   I saw three ships come sailing in
   On Christmas Day in the morning.

2. And what was in those ships all three,
   On Christmas Day, on Christmas Day?
   And what was in those ships all three,
   On Christmas Day in the morning?

3. Our Savior Christ and His Lady...
   (continue similarly)

4. Pray, whither sailed those ships all three?...

5. O, they sailed into Bethlehem...

6. And all the bells on earth shall ring...

7. And all the angels in Heav'n shall sing...

8. And all the souls on earth shall sing...

9. Then let us all rejoice amain...

JOLLY OLD ST. NICHOLAS 57

Traditional

1. Jolly old Saint Nicholas, lean your ear this way,
   Don't you tell a single soul what I'm going to say.
   Christmas Eve is coming soon,
   Now, you dear old man,
   Whisper what you'll bring to me,
   Tell me if you can.

2. When the clock is striking twelve
   And I'm fast asleep,
   Down the chimney broad and black
   With your pack you'll creep.
   All the stockings you will find
   Hanging in a row,
   Mine will be the shortest one,
   You'll be sure to know.

IT CAME UPON THE MIDNIGHT CLEAR . . 58

Words by Edmund Hamilton Sears
Music by Richard S. Willis

1. It came upon the midnight clear,
   That glorious song of old,
   From angels bending near the earth
   To touch their harps of gold:
   "Peace on the earth, good will to men
   From heaven's all gracious King!"
   The world in solemn stillness lay
   To hear the angels sing.

2. Still through the cloven skies they come
   With peaceful wings unfurled,
   And still their heavenly music floats
   O'er all the weary world:
   Above its sad and lowly plains
   They bend on hovering wing,
   And ever o'er its Babel sounds
   The blessed angels sing.

3. Yet with the woes of sin and strife
   The world has suffered long;
   Beneath the heavenly strain have rolled
   Two thousand years of wrong;
   And man, at war with man, hears not
   The tidings which they bring;
   O hush the noise, ye men of strife
   And hear the angels sing.

4. O ye, beneath life's crushing load,
   Whose forms are bending low
   Who toil along the climbing way
   With painful steps and slow.
   Look now! for glad and golden hours
   Come swiftly on the wing;
   O rest beside the weary road
   And hear the angels sing!

5. For lo! the days are hastening on,
   By prophet bards foretold,
   When with the ever-circling years
   Comes round the age of gold;
   When peace shall over all the earth
   Its ancient splendors fling,
   And the whole world send back the song
   Which now the angels sing.

JOY TO THE WORLD 60

Words by Isaac Watts
Music by Lowell Mason
(after George Frideric Handel)

1. Joy to the world! The Lord is come!
   Let earth receive her King.
   Let ev'ry heart prepare Him room,
   And heav'n and nature sing,
   And heav'n and nature sing,
   And heav'n and heav'n and nature sing.

2. Joy to the world! The Savior reigns;
   Let men their songs employ;
   While fields and floods,
   Rocks, hills and plains,
   Repeat the sounding joy,
   Repeat the sounding joy,
   Repeat, repeat the sounding joy.

3. He rules the world with truth and grace;
   And makes the nations prove
   The glories of His righteousness,
   And wonders of His love,
   And wonders of His love,
   And wonders, wonders of His love.

LO, HOW A ROSE E'ER BLOOMING 62

Words: 15th-Century German Carol
Music by Michael Praetorius

1. Lo, how a rose e'er blooming
   From tender stem hath sprung.
   Of Jesse's lineage coming,
   As men of old have sung.
   It came, a flower bright,
   Amid the cold of winter
   When half-spent was the night.

2. Isaiah 'twas foretold it,
   The rose I had in mind;
   With Mary we behold it,
   The Virgin, mother kind.
   To show God's love aright
   She bore to men a Savior
   When half-spent was the night.

O CHRISTMAS TREE 64

(O Tannenbaum)
Traditional German Carol

1. O Christmas tree, O Christmas tree,
   Thou tree most fair and lovely!
   O Christmas tree, O Christmas tree,
   Thou tree most fair and lovely!
   The sight of thee at Christmastide
   Spreads hope and gladness far and wide.
   O Christmas tree, O Christmas tree,
   Thou tree most fair and lovely!

2. O Christmas tree, O Christmas tree,
   Thou hast a wondrous message.
   O Christmas tree, O Christmas tree,
   Thou hast a wondrous message.
   Thou dost proclaim the Savior's birth,
   Good will to men and peace on earth.
   O Christmas tree, O Christmas tree,
   Thou hast a wondrous message.

UP ON THE HOUSETOP 65

Words and Music by Benjamin Hanby

1. Up on the housetop reindeer pause;
   Out jumps good old Santa Claus,
   Down through the chimney with lots of toys,
   All for the little ones' Christmas joys!

Ho, ho, ho, who wouldn't go?
Ho, ho, ho, who wouldn't go?
Up on the housetop, click, click, click,
Down through the chimney with good Saint Nick.

2. First comes the stocking of little Nell;
   Oh, dear Santa, fill it well;
   Give her a dolly that laughs and cries,
   One that can open and shut its eyes.

(Chorus)

3. Look in the stocking of little Bill;
   Oh, just see that glorious fill!
   Here is a hammer and lots of tacks,
   Whistle and ball and a set of jacks.

(Chorus)

O COME, ALL YE FAITHFUL 66

(Adeste Fideles)
Latin Words by John Francis Wade
English Translation by Frederick Oakeley
Music by John Francis Wade

1. O come, all ye faithful, joyful and triumphant,
   O come ye, O come ye to Bethlehem.
   Come and behold Him, born the King of angels.
   O come, let us adore Him;
   O come, let us adore Him;
   O come, let us adore Him, Christ, the Lord.

2. Sing, choirs of angels,
   Sing in exultation;
   Sing all ye citizens of heav'n above.
   Glory to God, all glory in the highest.
   O come, let us adore Him;
   O come, let us adore Him;
   O come, let us adore Him, Christ, the Lord.

3. Yea, Lord, we greet Thee,

Born this happy morning;
Jesus, to Thee be all glory giv'n;
Word of the Father, now in flesh appearing.
O come, let us adore Him;
O come, let us adore Him;
O come, let us adore Him, Christ, the Lord.

O COME, O COME, EMMANUEL 68

English Lyrics by John M. Neale
13th-Century Plainsong

1. O come, O come, Emmanuel
   And ransom captive Israel
   That mourns in lonely exile here
   Until the Son of God appear.
   Rejoice! Rejoice! Emmanuel
   Shall come to thee, O Israel.

2. O come, Thou Rod of Jesse, free
   Thine own from Satan's tyranny.
   From depths of hell thy people save,
   And give them vict'ry o'er the grave.
   Rejoice! Rejoice! Emmanuel
   Shall come to thee, O Israel.

3. O come, O Dayspring, come and cheer
   Our spirits by Thine advent here,
   And drive away the shades of night
   And pierce the clouds and bring us light.
   Rejoice! Rejoice! Emmanuel
   Shall come to thee, O Israel.

O LITTLE TOWN OF BETHLEHEM 70

Words by Phillips Brooks
Music by Lewis H. Redner

1. O little town of Bethlehem,
   How still we see thee lie!
   Above thy deep and dreamless sleep
   The silent stars go by.
   Yet in thy dark streets shineth
   The everlasting Light;
   The hopes and fears of all the years
   Are met in thee tonight.

2. For Christ is born of Mary,
   And gathered all above,
   While mortals sleep, the angels keep
   Their watch of wond'ring love.
   O morning stars together
   Proclaim the holy birth!
   And praises sing to God the King
   And peace to men on earth.

3. How silently, how silently
   The wond'rous gift is giv'n!
   So God imparts to human hearts

The blessings of His heav'n.
No ear may hear His coming,
But in this world of sin,
Where meek souls will receive Him still,
The dear Christ enters in.

4. Where children pure and happy
   Pray to the blessed Child,
   Where misery cries out to Thee,
   Son of the mother mild;
   Where charity stands watching
   And faith holds wide the door,
   The dark night wakes, the glory breaks,
   And Christmas comes once more.

5. O holy Child of Bethlehem,
   Descend to us we pray;
   Cast out our sin and enter in,
   Be born in us today.
   We hear the Christmas angels
   The great glad tidings tell;
   O come to us, abide with us,
   Our Lord, Immanuel.

RISE UP, SHEPHERD, AND FOLLOW 72

African-American Spiritual

Rise up, shepherd, and follow.
Rise up, shepherd, and follow.

1. There's a star in the East on Christmas morn;
   Rise up, shepherd, and follow.
   It will lead to the place where the Savior's born;
   Rise up, shepherd, and follow.
   Follow, follow, rise up, shepherd, and follow;
   Follow the star of Bethlehem;
   Rise up, shepherd, and follow.

2. If you take good heed to the angel's words;
   Rise up, shepherd, and follow.
   You'll forget your flocks, you'll forget your herds;
   Rise up, shepherd, and follow.
   Follow, follow, rise up, shepherd, and follow;
   Follow the star of Bethlehem;
   Rise up, shepherd, and follow.

Oh yes, rise up, shepherd, rise up, shepherd,
Rise up, shepherd, and follow.

WE THREE KINGS OF ORIENT ARE 74

Words and Music by
John Henry Hopkins, Jr.

1. We three kings of Orient are
   Bearing gifts we traverse afar.
   Fields and fountain, moor and mountain,
   Following yonder star.

   O star of wonder, star of night,
   Star with royal beauty bright,
   Westward leading, still proceeding,
   Guide us to thy perfect light.

2. Born a King on Bethlehem's plain,
   Gold I bring to crown Him again.
   King forever, ceasing never,
   Over us all to reign.
   (Chorus)

3. Frankincense to offer have I,
   Incense owns a Deity nigh.
   Pray'r and praising, all men raising,
   Worship Him, God most high.
   (Chorus)

4. Myrrh is mine, its bitter perfume
   Breathes a life of gathering gloom;
   Sorrowing, sighing, bleeding, dying,
   Sealed in the stone-cold tomb.
   (Chorus)

5. Glorious now behold Him arise,
   King and God and Sacrifice.
   Alleluia, Alleluia,
   Earth to heav'n replies.
   (Chorus)

WHAT CHILD IS THIS? 76

Words by William Chatterton Dix
16th-Century English Melody ("Greensleeves")

1. What Child is this, who laid to rest
   On Mary's lap is sleeping?
   Whom angels greet with anthems sweet,
   While shepherds watch are keeping?
   This, this is Christ the King,
   Whom shepherds guard and angels sing:
   Haste, haste to bring Him laud,
   The Babe, the Son of Mary.

2. Why lies He in such mean estate,
   Where ox and ass are feeding?
   Good Christian, fear, for sinners here
   The silent word is pleading.
   Nails, spear shall pierce Him through,
   The cross be borne for me, for you:
   Hail, hail, the Word made flesh,
   The Babe, the Son of Mary.

3. So bring Him incense, gold and myrrh,
   Come peasant, king, to own Him.
   The King of Kings salvation brings;
   Let loving hearts enthrone Him.
   Raise, raise the song on high,
   The Virgin sings her lullaby:
   Joy, joy, for Christ is born,
   The Babe, the Son of Mary.

THE TWELVE DAYS OF CHRISTMAS 78

Traditional

1. On the first day of Christmas
   My true love sent to me
   A partridge in a pear tree.

2. On the second day of Christmas
   My true love sent to me
   Two turtle doves
   And a partridge in a pear tree.

3. On the third day of Christmas
   My true love sent to me
   Three French hens, two turtle doves
   And a partridge in a pear tree.

4. On the fourth day of Christmas
   My true love sent to me
   Four calling birds, three French hens,
   Two turtle doves
   And a partridge in a pear tree.

5. On the fifth day of Christmas
   My true love sent to me
   Five golden rings, four calling birds,
   Three French hens, two turtle doves
   And a partridge in a pear tree.

6. On the sixth day of Christmas
   My true love sent to me
   Six geese a-laying, five golden rings,
   Four calling birds, three French hens,
   Two turtle doves and a partridge in a pear tree.

7. On the seventh day of Christmas
   My true love sent to me
   Seven swans a-swimming, six geese a-laying,
   Five golden rings, four calling birds,
   Three French hens, two turtle doves
   And a partridge in a pear tree.

8. On the eighth day of Christmas
   My true love sent to me
   Eight maids a-milking, seven swans a-swimming,
   Six geese a-laying, five golden rings,
   Four calling birds, three French hens,
   Two turtle doves and a partridge in a pear tree.

9. On the ninth day of Christmas
   My true love sent to me
   Nine ladies dancing, eight maids a-milking,
   Seven swans a-swimming, six geese a-laying,
   Five golden rings, four calling birds,
   Three French hens, two turtle doves
   And a partridge in a pear tree.

10. On the tenth day of Christmas
    My true love sent to me
    Ten lords a-leaping, nine ladies dancing,
    Eight maids a-milking, seven swans a-swim-
    ming,
    Six geese a-laying, five golden rings,
    Four calling birds, three French hens,
    Two turtle doves and a partridge in a pear tree.

11. On the 'leventh day of Christmas
    My true love sent to me
    Eleven pipers piping, ten lords a-leaping,
    Nine ladies dancing, eight maids a-milking,
    Seven swans a-swimming, six geese a-laying,
    Five golden rings, four calling birds,
    Three French hens, two turtle doves
    And a partridge in a pear tree.

12. On the twelfth day of Christmas
    My true love sent to me
    Twelve drummers drumming, 'leven pipers
    piping,
    Ten lords a-leaping, nine ladies dancing,
    Eight maids a-milking, seven swans a-swim-
    ming,
    Six geese a-laying, five golden rings,
    Four calling birds, three French hens,
    Two turtle doves and a partridge in a pear tree.

A CHILDREN'S CHRISTMAS

RUDOLPH, THE RED-NOSED REINDEER .. 81

Words and Music by
Johnny Marks

You know Dasher and Dancer and Prancer and Vixen,
Comet and Cupid and Donner and Blitzen.
But do you recall the most famous reindeer of all?

Rudolph, the Red-Nosed Reindeer
Had a very shiny nose,
And if you ever saw it,
You would even say it glows.
All of the other reindeer
Used to laugh and call him names;
They never let poor Rudolph
Join in any reindeer games.

Then one foggy Christmas Eve,
Santa came to say:
"Rudolph, with your nose so bright,
Won't you guide my sleigh tonight?"

Then how the reindeer loved him,
As they shouted out with glee:
"Rudolph, the Red-Nosed Reindeer,
You'll go down in history!"

FROSTY THE SNOWMAN. 84

Words and Music by
Steve Nelson and Jack Rollins

Frosty the Snowman was a jolly, happy soul,
With a corncob pipe and a button nose
And two eyes made out of coal.
Frosty the Snowman is a fairy tale, they say,
He was made of snow but the children know
How he came to life one day.

There must have been some magic
In that old silk hat they found,
For when they placed it on his head
He began to dance around. Oh,

Frosty the Snowman was alive as he could be,
And the children say he could laugh and play
Just the same as you and me.

Frosty the Snowman knew the sun was hot that day,
So he said, "Let's run and we'll have some fun,
Now before I melt away."
Down to the village with a broomstick in his hand,
Running here and there all around the square,
Sayin' "Catch me if you can!"

He led them down the streets of town
Right to the traffic cop.
And he only paused a moment when
He heard him holler "Stop!" For
Frosty the Snowman had to hurry on his way,
But he waved goodbye sayin' "Don't you cry,
I'll be back again someday!"

Thumpety thump thump, thumpety thump thump,
Look at Frosty go;
Thumpety thump thump, thumpety thump thump,
Over the fields of snow.

ALL THROUGH THE NIGHT
Traditional Welsh Carol

1. Sleep, my Child and peace attend Thee
   All through the night.
   Guardian angels God will send Thee
   All through the night.
   Soft the drowsy hours are creeping,
   Hill and vale in slumber sleeping,
   God His loving vigil keeping
   All through the night.

2. While the moon her watch is keeping
   All through the night;
   While the weary world is sleeping
   All through the night.
   Through your dreams you're swiftly stealing,
   Visions of delight revealing,
   Christmas time is so appealing
   All through the night.

3. You, my God, a Babe of wonder
   All through the night;
   Dreams you dream can't break from thunder
   All through the night.
   Children's dreams cannot be broken,
   Life is but a lovely token.
   Christmas should be softly spoken
   All through the night.

SUZY SNOWFLAKE
Words and Music by
Sid Tepper and Roy C. Bennett

Here comes Suzy Snowflake
Dressed in a snow-white gown,
Tap, tap, tappin' at your window pane
To tell you she's in town.
Here comes Suzy Snowflake,
Soon you will hear her say:
Come out ev'ryone and play with me,
I haven't long to stay.

If you wanna make a snowman,
I'll help you make one, one, two, three.
If you wanna take a sleigh ride,
The ride's on me!

Here comes Suzy Snowflake,
Look at her tumblin' down,
Bringing joy to ev'ry girl and boy;
Suzy's come to town.

TOYLAND
Words by Glen MacDonough
Music by Victor Herbert

Toyland, Toyland, little girl and boy land.
While you dwell within it you are ever happy then.
Childhood's joyland, mystic merry Toyland,
Once you pass its borders you can ne'er return
again.

THE FRIENDLY BEASTS
Traditional

1. Jesus, our Brother kind and good
   Was humbly born in a stable rude.
   And the friendly beasts around Him stood,
   Jesus, our Brother kind and good.

2. "I," said the donkey, shaggy and brown,
   "I carried His mother up hill and down;
   I carried her safely to Bethlehem town.
   I," said the donkey, shaggy and brown.

3. "I," said the cow, all white and red,
   "I gave Him my manger for a bed;
   I gave Him my hay to pillow His head.
   I," said the cow, all white and red.

4. "I," said the sheep with curly horn,
   "I gave Him my wool for His blanket warm;
   He wore my coat on Christmas morn.
   I," said the sheep with curly horn.

5. "I," said the dove from the rafters high,
   "Cooed Him to sleep that He should not cry;
   We cooed Him to sleep, my mate and I.
   I," said the dove from the rafters high.

6. "I," said the camel, yellow and black,
   "Over the desert, upon my back
   I brought Him a gift in the Wise Men's pack.
   I," said the camel, yellow and black.

7. Thus every beast by some good spell
   In the stable dark was glad to tell
   Of the gift he gave Emmanuel,
   The gift he gave Emmanuel.

AWAY IN A MANGER
Words: Anonymous (stanzas 1, 2)
*   John Thomas McFarland (stanza 3)*
Music by James R. Murray

1. Away in a manger, no crib for a bed,
   The little Lord Jesus laid down His sweet head.
   The stars in the sky looked down where He lay,
   The little Lord Jesus asleep on the hay.

2. The cattle are lowing, the poor Baby wakes,
   But little Lord Jesus, no crying He makes.
   I love Thee, Lord Jesus, look down from the sky,
   And stay by my cradle till morning is nigh.

3. Be near me, Lord Jesus, I ask Thee to stay
   Close by me forever, and love me, I pray.
   Bless all the dear children in Thy tender care,
   And take us to heaven to live with Thee there.

CHRISTMAS WITH A SMILE

GRANDMA GOT RUN OVER
Words and Music by
Randy Brooks

Grandma got run over by a reindeer
Walking home from our house Christmas Eve.
You can say there's no such thing as Santa,
But as for me and Grandpa, we believe.

1. She'd been drinking too much eggnog
   And we begged her not to go,
   But she forgot her medication,
   And she staggered out the door into the snow.
   When we found her Christmas morning
   At the scene of the attack,
   She had footprints on her forehead,
   And incriminating Claus marks on her back.

(Chorus)

2. Now we're all so proud of Grandpa,
   He's been taking this so well.
   See him in there watching football,
   Drinking beer and playing cards with cousin Mel.
   It's not Christmas without Grandma,
   All the fam'ly's dressed in black,
   And we just can't help but wonder:
   Should we open up her gifts or send them back.

(Chorus)

3. Now the goose is on the table,
   And the pudding made of fig,
   And the blue and silver candles
   That would just have matched the hair
   In Grandma's wig.
   I've warned all my friends and neighbors,
   Better watch out for yourselves,
   They should never give a license
   To a man who drives a sleigh and plays with elves.

(Chorus)

ALL I WANT FOR CHRISTMAS
Words and Music by
Don Gardner

All I want for Christmas is my two front teeth,
My two front teeth, see my two front teeth.
Gee, if I could only have my two front teeth,
Then I could wish you "Merry Christmas."
It seems so long since I could say,
"Sister Susie sitting on a thistle."
Gosh, oh gee, how happy I'd be
If I could only whistle. *(thhh)*
All I want for Christmas is my two front teeth,
My two front teeth, see my two front teeth.
Gee, if I could only have my two front teeth,
Then I could wish you "Merry Christmas."

WELCOME CHRISTMAS (from *The Grinch*) . . 100
Lyrics by Dr. Seuss
Music by Albert Hague

Fah who foraze! Dah who doraze!
Welcome Christmas, come this way!
Fah who foraze! Dah who doraze!
Welcome Christmas, Christmas Day!
Welcome, welcome! Fah who rahmus!
Welcome, welcome! Dah who dahmus!
Christmas Day is in our grasp!
So long as we have hands to clasp!
Fah who foraze! Dah who doraze!
Welcome Christmas! Bring your cheer.
Welcome all who's far and near.

Fah who foraze! Dah who doraze!
Welcome Christmas, come this way!
Fah who foraze! Dah who doraze!
Welcome Christmas, Christmas Day!
Welcome, Christmas! Fah who rahmus!
Welcome, Christmas! Dah who dahmus!
Christmas Day will always be
Just as long as we have we!
Fah who foraze! Dah who doraze!
Welcome Christmas! Bring your cheer.
Welcome all who's far and near.

Nuttin' for Christmas 102

Words and Music by
Sid Tepper and Roy C. Bennett

I broke my bat on Johnny's head;
Somebody snitched on me.
I hid a frog in sister's bed;
Somebody snitched on me.
I spilled some ink on Mommy's rug,
I made Tommy eat a bug,
Bought some gum with a penny slug;
Somebody snitched on me. Oh,

I'm gettin' nuttin' for Christmas,
Mommy and Daddy are mad.
I'm gettin' nuttin' for Christmas;
'Cause I ain't been nuttin' but bad.

I put a tack on teacher's chair;
Somebody snitched on me.
I tied a knot in Susie's hair;
Somebody snitched on me.
I did a dance on Mommy's plants,
Climbed a tree and tore my pants,
Filled the sugar bowl with ants;
Somebody snitched on me. So,

I'm gettin' nuttin' for Christmas;
Mommy and Daddy are mad.
I'm gettin' nuttin' for Christmas,
'Cause I ain't been nuttin' but bad.

I won't be seeing Santa Claus;
Somebody snitched on me.
He won't come visit me because
Somebody snitched on me.
Next year I'll be going straight,
Next year I'll be good, just wait!
I'd start now but it's too late.
Somebody snitched on me. Oh,

I'm gettin' nuttin' for Christmas;
Mommy and Daddy are mad.
I'm gettin' nuttin' for Christmas,
'Cause I ain't been nuttin' but bad.

So you better be good, whatever you do,
'Cause if you're bad I'm warning you,
You'll get nuttin' for Christmas.

GREAT COMPOSERS LOOK AT CHRISTMAS

Sleigh Ride 105

Words by Mitchell Parish
Music by Leroy Anderson

Just hear those sleigh bells jingling,
Ring-ting-tingling too.
Come on, it's lovely weather
For a sleigh ride together with you.
Outside the snow is falling and
Friends are calling "Yoo-hoo!"
Come on, it's lovely weather
For a sleigh ride together with you.

Giddy-yap, giddy-yap, giddy-yap, let's go,
Let's look at the snow,
We're riding in a wonderland of snow.
Giddy-yap, giddy-yap, giddy-yap, it's grand,
Just holding your hand.
We're gliding along with a song
Of a wintery fairyland.
Our cheeks are nice and rosy,
And comfy cozy are we.
We're snuggled up together
Like two birds of a feather would be.
Let's take that road before us
And sing a chorus or two.
Come on, it's lovely weather
For a sleigh ride together with you.

Gesú Bambino 112

(The Infant Jesus)
Words and Music by
Pietro A. Yon

When blossoms flowered 'mid the snows
Upon a winter night
Was born the Child, the Christmas Rose,
The King of love and light.
The angels sang, the shepherds sang,
The grateful earth rejoiced.
And at His blessed birth the stars
Their exultation voiced:
O come, let us adore Him;
O come, let us adore Him;
O come, let us adore Him, Christ, the Lord.

Again the heart with rapture glows
To greet the holy night

That gave the world its Christmas Rose,
The King of love and light.
Let ev'ry voice acclaim His name,
The grateful chorus dwell.
From paradise to earth He came
That we with Him might dwell:
O come, let us adore Him;
O come, let us adore Him;
O come, let us adore Him, Christ, the Lord.

I HEARD THE BELLS ON CHRISTMAS DAY 114

Words by Henry Wadsworth Longfellow
Music by Jean Baptiste Calkin

1. I heard the bells on Christmas Day,
   Their old familiar carols play.
   And mild and sweet the words repeat
   Of peace on earth, good will to men.

2. I thought how, as the day had come,
   The belfries of all Christendom
   Had rolled along th'unbroken song
   Of peace on earth, good will to men.

3. And in despair I bow'd my head:
   "There is no peace on earth," I said,
   "For hate is strong, and mocks the song
   Of peace on earth, good will to men."

4. Then pealed the bells more loud and deep:
   "God is not dead, nor doth He sleep;
   The wrong shall fail, the right prevail,
   With peace on earth, good will to men."

5. Till, ringing, singing on its way,
   The world revolved from night to day,
   A voice, a chime, a chant sublime,
   Of peace on earth, good will to men!

O HOLY NIGHT 115

(Cantique de Noël)
Words by Placide Cappeau
English Translation by John Sullivan Dwight
Music by Adolphe Charles Adam

1. O holy night, the stars are brightly shining;
   It is the night of the dear Savior's birth.
   Long lay the world in sin and error pining
   Till He appeared and the soul felt its worth.
   A thrill of hope, the weary world rejoices,
   For yonder breaks a new and glorious morn.
   Fall on your knees, O hear the angel voices!
   O night divine, O night when Christ was born!
   O night, O holy night, O night divine.

2. Led by the light of faith serenely beaming,
   With glowing hearts by His cradle we stand.
   So led by light of a star sweetly gleaming,
   Here came the wise men from the Orient land.
   The King of Kings lay in lowly manger,
   In all our trials born to be our friend.
   He knows our need, to our weakness no stranger.
   Behold your King! before Him lowly bend!
   Behold your King! your King! before him bend.

3. Truly He taught us to love one another;
   His law is love and His gospel is peace.
   Chains shall He break, for the slave is our brother,
   And in His name all oppression shall cease.
   Sweet hymns of joy in grateful chorus raise we,
   Let all within us praise His holy name.
   Christ is the Lord, then ever, ever praise we!
   His power and glory evermore proclaim!
   His pow'r and glory evermore proclaim.

A ROCKIN' CHRISTMAS

ROCKIN' AROUND THE CHRISTMAS TREE 118

Words and Music by
Johnny Marks

Rockin' around the Christmas tree
At the Christmas party hop,
Mistletoe hung where you can see;
Ev'ry couple tries to stop.
Rockin' around the Christmas tree,
Let the Christmas spirit ring.
Later we'll have some pumpkin pie
And we'll do some caroling.

You will get a sentimental feeling when you hear
Voices singing, "Let's be jolly;
Deck the halls with boughs of holly."
Rockin' around the Christmas tree,
Have a happy holiday.
Ev'ryone dancing merrily
In the new old-fashioned way.

JINGLE BELL ROCK

Words and Music by
Joe Beal and Jim Boothe

Jingle-bell, jingle-bell, jingle-bell rock,
Jingle-bell swing, and jingle-bells ring.
Snowin' and blowin' up bushels of fun
Now the jingle-hop has begun.
Jingle-bell, jingle-bell, jingle-bell rock,
Jingle-bells chime in jingle-bell time;
Dancin' and prancin' in Jingle-Bell Square
In the frosty air.

What a bright time, it's the right time
To rock the night away.
Jingle-bell time is a swell time
To go glidin' in a one-horse sleigh.

Giddy up jingle-horse pick up your feet,
Jingle around the clock;
Mix and mingle in a jinglin' beat.
That's the jingle-bell,
That's the jingle-bell,
That's the jingle-bell rock.

AND A HAPPY NEW YEAR

AULD LANG SYNE

Words by Robert Burns
Music: Traditional Scottish Melody

1. Should auld acquaintance be forgot
   And never brought to mind?
   Should auld acquaintance be forgot
   And days of auld lang syne?
   For auld lang syne, my dear, for auld lang syne;
   We'll take a cup of kindness yet for
   auld lang syne.

2. And here's a hand, my trusty friend,
   And gives a hand o' thine,
   We'll take a cup of kindness yet for
   auld lang syne.
   For auld lang syne, my dear, for auld lang syne;
   We'll take a cup of kindness yet for
   auld lang syne.

WE WISH YOU A MERRY CHRISTMAS

Traditional

1. We wish you a Merry Christmas,
   We wish you a Merry Christmas,
   We wish you a Merry Christmas,
   And a Happy New Year.
   Good tidings to you wherever you are;
   Good tidings for Christmas
   And a happy New Year.

2. Oh, bring us a figgy pudding,
   Oh, bring us a figgy pudding,
   Oh, bring us a figgy pudding,
   And a cup of good cheer.
   Good tidings to you wherever you are;
   Good tidings for Christmas
   And a Happy New Year.

3. We won't go until we've got some,
   We won't go until we've got some,
   We won't go until we've got some,
   So bring some out here.
   Good tidings to you wherever you are;
   Good tidings for Christmas
   And a Happy New Year.

4. We wish you a Merry Christmas,
   We wish you a Merry Christmas,
   We wish you a Merry Ch ristmas,
   And a Happy New Year.